A REAL LIFE

A REAL LIFE

Restoring What Matters:
Family, Good Friends, and a True Community

FERENC MÁTÉ

Albatross Books

at

W. W. Norton & Company

New York • London

DEDICATION

For those of us who believe a better life is within reach.

CONTENTS

AUTHOR'S NOTE

WE SEEM TO have forgotten what life is all about. Inundated by sound-bites, ad-campaigns, hyperlinks, special effects, and messages texted and twittered, we rarely have time to address our most vital, deeply-rooted needs. Driven to distraction by this mostly meaningless information, we have created a culture in which not only is our financial future insecure—the President of France called it "a house of cards"—and our planet endangered, but we ourselves are becoming electronic exiles, living with our gadgets, lonely in vast crowds.

It is no accident that depression in its many manifestations—physical and emotional—has become a global epidemic.

Once we accept this, we can begin to fix what is broken. One might ask, "How can you tackle all these aspects together? Why not concentrate on fixing just one?" Unfortunately, our world is not only fragile but also interdependent; like a bicycle wheel whose spokes are delicate and manifold. When the wheel is badly bent, it's not enough to fix just one spoke, for we will still end up wobbling hopelessly along.

The necessary repairs can't come from the top—there really is no top we can believe in anymore—the effort has to come from those who brought this on our heads: us.

The first step is to delve into what compels us. Why do we live the way we do? Why do we strive? For what? For whom?

The second step is to find a better way.

While the undertaking requires change, its beauty is that there is no piper to pay, cross to bear or bullet to bite. The solution to a better life involves no hardship: all we need to do is *lead* a better life. This simply means doing work that offers true pleasure and security; eating and playing in a way that yields health and sensory gratification; and having relationships that bring us joy, trust, loyalty and satisfaction.

Throughout the book I use U.S. references not to single out America, but because its studies and statistics are the most abundant and thorough. And to have any hope of success, a movement needs a wide base. There is no other country in the world that can rally behind a cause with either the required size or zeal. Furthermore, having a new idea is just step one; the bigger task is selling it to the world. America has been an expert at marketing its values: lifestyle, abundance, gadgets, and entertainment. Now, it alone can bring the swift change needed: deleting all of the above, and letting us live securely, with greater fulfillment, more creativity, face to face, with a helluva lot more passion.

"Whatever you can do or dream, you can begin it. Boldness has genius, power and magic in it. Begin it now."

—GOETHE

CHAPTER 1

The Pursuit of Happiness

"If only we'd stop trying to be happy
we'd have a pretty good time."

—EDITH WHARTON

THE MOST UNIVERSALLY admired part of the
United States Declaration of Independence, penned by
the Founding Fathers and adopted by Congress on July
4, 1776, reads:

"We hold these Truths to be self-evident, that all Men
are created equal, that they are endowed by their Cre-
ator with certain unalienable Rights, that among these
are Life, Liberty and the pursuit of Happiness."

That noble sentence had but one oversight; while the
meaning of "Life" and "Liberty" is pretty "self-evi-

dent," most of us haven't the faintest clue of what they meant by "Happiness," or why, even more bafflingly, it has to be pursued, like some mischievous puppy that ran off with your slippers.

For decades we were convinced that happiness was the American Dream in which even a child of two had his own flat screen TV, where nearly every family owned a half-empty McMansion, at least one SUV, and an RV rooted firmly in the driveway; where we could sing in our underwear and make twenty million dollars, or whack a ball over the fence and make forty; or, if we traded our minds in for a pocket calculator, we could put our name on hotels and skyscrapers, and have a TV show teaching apprentice barracudas, and no one would say to our faces that a double comb-over is an indisputable sign of being terminally crazy.

In short, we all seemed to have been part of a silent conspiracy in which we agreed that the Founding Fathers had blown it, and through a slip of the pen wrote "Happiness" when they actually meant "Money." We felt Joan Rivers spoke for us all when she quipped, "People say that money is not the key to happiness, but I always figured if you have enough money, you can have a key made."

So we all chased wealth while we largely neglected, or considered secondary, the health of our ideals, the nourishment of our children's minds and bodies, the honesty and integrity of our institutions of government and religion, the safety of our infrastructures, hospitals and schools, the strength of our social fabric, of our neighborhoods and family, and that much–maligned stepchild—whose air, water and soil are the essence of all life—our environment.

While some of us found these neglects profoundly disturbing, we kept our mental equilibrium by pointing with pride at our standard of living thanks to a robust economy. But now that the economy has been flushed down the toilet, and is on its way to some white sand beach where it will sit next to tar-balls from oil spills, and undereducated bimbos, perhaps the time has come to ask, "What the hell do we do now?"

The world has envied and embraced whatever we North Americans dreamed up from junk food to junk bonds, from i-this and i-that to five dollar coffee in a paper cup. It seems it's time we dream up, a different kind of dream because mindless mass production and mass consumption seem to be leading us to social, environmental and economic dead ends. Perhaps it's time to admit to ourselves that despite our giant cars and houses—both of which are twice as big as Grandpa's when he was young—and despite our pants and U-Store-Its bursting at the seams, we are not one iota happier, but much more frantic than dear Grandpa.

Perhaps it's time to sit down for a good heart-to-heart with the one person who can really make a difference:

our self. Perhaps it's time to ask a few unnerving questions like what *really* counts in life. What is true success? Is it the heft of our portfolio or the irrepressible laughter of our children? What makes us feel secure, proud, or fulfilled, and when, if ever, do we feel truly independent? Maybe we should re-examine our sacred cows: our jobs and careers; houses and neighborhoods; the way we make our foods and the way we eat them; our system of democracy that admittedly yields the best politicians money can buy; how we spend our free time, what we call entertainment; how we really want to live; and what we'd like to leave behind when we die. The answers might just lead us to a calmer way of life centered on our communities, with our family, *real* friends, and where "Happiness" will no longer need to be "pursued," but will be all around us, like the air.

Think about the lines of W. Beran Wolfe, who in the 1930s wrote, "If you observe a really happy man you will find him building a boat, writing a symphony, educating his son, growing double dahlias in his garden. He will not be searching for happiness as if it were a collar button that has rolled under the radiator."

MY NEW SHORTER Oxford English Dictionary defines happiness as "deep pleasure in, or contentment with, one's circumstances."

Through much of history, we humans were a simple

lot whose pleasures and fulfillment came from two basic sources: the natural world around us and each other. Both were available at no cost and in limitless supply.

We knew and understood our world: plants and animals, seasons and rains, knew how they could feed us, knew how they could hurt us. Nature's ever-changing beauty fascinated us; her mysteries in turn terrified and thrilled us.

Meanwhile, people—friends, family, co-workers, neighbors—were by and large the highlights of our lives. Whether on a stroll down a village street or at a Sunday picnic, or an evening in the town square, on a park bench or in a bar; or having a game of cards at the kitchen table; or just sitting and gossiping in front of our caves, on our front porches, we were happy to be together, to exchange lousy jokes and great ideas, to share good times and bad, to enjoy each other's company.

And our fulfillment, whether material or emotional, came often from ourselves. We took pride in what we made with our hands: grew, hunted, or cobbled together in the home, in the meal we cooked from scratch, in clothing we weaved, sewed or knitted.

But since the seventies or eighties, our attention and our passions seemed to have veered. We diverted our compass course away from relationships, from humanity, from both nature and people, and away, most notably, from the work of our own two hands, toward a perpetually zealous, nearly worshipful accumulation of goods: gear, gadgets and trinkets. Things. And they weren't things that we thought up, or grew, or cooked, or made, but things that we merely paid for. Bought.

When we weren't buying or working toward buying, or thinking about buying, we filled what time was left with things that *pretended* to be real life and real people: television, video games and electronic friends. The real people, the ones you could touch and hug, seemed to vanish from our lives, replaced by the "virtual"—which is the virtual word for fake.

You could at this point shrug your shoulders and say, "So what? That's progress, things change. The strong survive." And I'm the first to admit that it's a daunting task to try and weigh the benefits of this sea change against the damage it has done. But since, as most of us sense in our heart of hearts, we are in a profound state of economic and social disillusion, this might be the perfect time to look at the way we live and compare our modern, virtual existence to the one that, for millennia, we called Life.

The aim is not to find fault but, rather, to first comprehend what has taken place, and then to rediscover and recapture the simple joys we've lost; the happiness and fulfillment we once found—without web surfing or pursuit—in our daily lives.

CHAPTER 2

Time *Was* On Our Side

"Time you enjoyed wasting is not wasted time."
—BERTRAND RUSSELL

BEFORE WE SET out to find a new American Dream,
it's best to invent a new American clock, one that keeps
a more easygoing time. It could be a simpler version of
current time pieces, indicating no seconds or minutes,
just hours. It might seem normal now that our frantic lives be measured in tiny fragments—recently, in a
stroke of hyper madness, the NHL retooled their game
clocks to show hundredths of a second—but, not long
ago, we were content to know time more or less.

A few decades back, we lost a friend that might have
helped to preserve our sanity: the Grandfather Clock.
For those unversed in old Dracula movies, the clock was

man-height, with a two-foot-long pendulum that swung back and forth, and made a sound that was undeniably "tick-tock." Once in a while it would chime the precise hour, reminding us that a precious part of our life had passed.

But Grandfather Clocks ticked their last tock years ago, during the same epoch in which we lost a wondrous place: the front porch: a structure of endless magic in whose rocking chair or creaky wicker sofa we could collapse and make time stand still. While the Grandfather clock reminded us of the value of each hour, the front porch allowed us to fully live it. We could sit there and hum or read, gaze off in the distance or at the girl across the street, peel potatoes, crack walnuts or spit watermelon seeds over the fence, or we could chat with neighbors passing by, tell stories, make up lies, or just lean back, stare at the sky and dream.

For much of our history as a species, we lived by the seasons, rose with the chickens and went to bed with the sun. We were never late for anything because no one measured time.

That was before our lives were permanently stuck on Fast Forward. Long before money-obsessed men ruled the world and invented terms like "downtime," "kill time," "quality time," "time management" and the idiom that sounds like fingernails on a blackboard: "time is money."

Were that phrase uttered somewhat earlier in our history, God would have quickly changed his bumper sticker from "Be fruitful and multiply," to "Get thee a vasectomy!"

But God blinked, and the inventor of the phrase went forth and multiplied, littering the neighborhood with emotionally blinkered runts who now largely run our lives making us frantically strut, fret, hurry, worry, Twitter, flitter and quickstep, to this nauseating global anthem.

ANCIENT GREEKS WERE satisfied with living by the sundial—the pleasures of the night were untouched by Time. It was the Christian monks of the Middle Ages who invented the mechanical clock to mark not only hours but every passing minute. Ironically, those who did nothing all day felt a dire need to do it precisely on schedule. From that moment, we were doomed; it was but a wee step to train schedules, the 9 to 5 grind, 24/7, multitasking, 401K's, two-week vacations, and the Two Minute Warning.

To the idea of Time, someone added Space, which meant that not only did you have to get up at an ungodly hour, but that, by the stroke of nine, you had to be *in the office* and in your cubicle.

We should have stuck with the earliest recorded Western philosophy of Time, noted by the ancient Egyptian thinker Ptahhotep (c. 2650–2600 BC), who was infinitely chill in reminding us, "Do not lessen the time of following desire, for the wasting of time is an abomination to the spirit." If you read his message closely, the word that stands out is "desire," and I'm sure he didn't mean lusting for a donut.

Ptahhotep's philosophy was recently amended by Lehman Brothers, who replaced "desire" with "mortgage-backed securities" and "collateralized debt obligations." They should have settled for the donut.

A more humane appreciation of Time came from an unexpected source. Those we associate with Haiku poetry, serious contemplation, magnificent gardens and the salmon-skin hand roll, invented my favorite proverb: "Time spent laughing is time spent with the Gods."

And, just as surprisingly, the best assimilated thought on Time comes not from a philosopher or writer but a painter. Georgia O'Keefe sadly remarked: "Nobody sees a flower—really—it is so small it takes time—we haven't time—and to see takes time, like to have a friend takes time."

So, first, let's stop the clock. Then spend long afternoons, *Sitting on the dock of the bay, watching the tide roll away. Wasting time.*

CHAPTER 3

Sunday, Lovely Sunday

JUST HOW MUCH we have mutated in a mere generation is perhaps best exemplified by what has happened
to our Sundays.

Not so long ago, our Sundays were devoted to flesh and
blood people; the Sunday family drive, family picnic or dinner, and the Sunday visit with neighbors and friends were
as American as apple pie. But that all changed. We have
replaced people with material goods to such an extent, that
the former US President no longer referred to his compa-
triots as "friends," or "fellow Americans," "Romans," or
"even "countrymen," but simply, and unapologetically as
"consumers." And consumers we have become; 24/7.

Whereas Sunday was once for restocking our minds
with fresh thoughts, insights and good conversations, for
restocking our spirit and our imagination, it has lately
become a day for restocking our closets. We once took
nature walks in the revitalizing beauty of the sunbathed

countryside, but we now walk mostly through the fluorescent light of the Mall. Or worse, we let our fingers
do the walking on our keyboards to virtual stores where
there is no day or night, and certainly no Sunday.

Most cultures acknowledge the need for a Sunday.
Whether it's called Sabbath or *Domenica*, or as Emperor
Constantine declared it in 321 AD, *Dies Solis*, the Day
of the Sun, it had been a day when "the magistrates
and people residing in cities rest, and all workshops
remain closed." And it was viewed "not just a holy
day of rest...but a Utopian idea about a less pressured,
more sociable, purer world."

For the religious, the explanation was, "We rest
because God rested on the seventh day...We rest in order
to honor the Divine in us, to remind ourselves that there
is more to us than just what we do during the week."

The secular believed: "The Sabbath is to the week
what the line break is to poetic language. It is the silence
that forces you to return to what came before and find
its meaning."

I'm not advocating the declaration of recluse Sundays
or - heaven forbid - a return to the Connecticut Blue
Laws of the eighteenth century which, besides forbid-
ding everything, prohibited kissing your baby, playing
an instrument or telling a joke. But after a week of hectic yet mostly passive work, which for the bulk of us
involves sitting at a computer, can we not feel our body
and soul crying out for something completely different?

We used to leave the house and get physical on Sundays: hike, walk, bike, or play scrub baseball or touch football at the park, but now we spend inert internet hours adrift in a virtual world, or veg'ing out in front of the tube—the average adult for four hours, even on Sunday. By passing up physical exertion, not only do we rob ourselves of healthy exercise but also miss refreshing our brain with endorphins, "happy hormones," which yield a feeling of well-being and even euphoria.

When we do move, it's with the militant logistics of our workweek, hence, just as stressful; whether it's Soccer Sunday or Little League Sunday, there is much planning and long hours of commute. And the sports our children play are no longer centered on socializing, sportsmanship, friendship or pure enjoyment, but, rather, one obsession: winning.

The Shopping Sunday is no better. While it might require a bit of movement, the stress of shopping is much like the stress of work, often worse—at work we can calm ourselves with the thought of making money, but shopping just casts us deeper into the anxiety of debt.

So the Sunday break is no break at all. Instead of being, for at least one day, not the consumer we have been trained to be but the person we really *want* to be; instead of separating ourselves from the demands of daily life; we simply dance the same old dance, sing another tired verse of the same old song.

It might behoove us to reflect on a eighteenth century

quote from Elijah of Vilna. "What we create becomes meaningful to us only once we stop creating it and start to think about why we did so. The implication is clear. We could let the world wind us up and set us marching, like mechanical dolls that go and go until they fall over, because they don't have a mechanism that allows them to pause. But that would make us less human. We have to remember to stop, because we have to stop to remember."

Lazin' on a Sunday Afternoon

As a kid, I used to wake up Sunday mornings when Tommy Flint next door yelled at the short fat dog he was trying to turn into a valiant Lassie. When Tommy leapt over the fence and ordered him to follow, Fat Dog just shook his head, ambled to a post, sniffed, and then had himself a little pee. That's when Tommy went ballistic and shook me from my dreams. Later his dad Ernie would shuffle over in his worn-out slippers, bum a cigarette from my mom, set himself down at the kitchen table, and nibble what was left of breakfast. While he discussed with my dad his garden or his Buick, my mom began cooking one of her epic Sunday meals.

Ours was a modest, working class Vancouver neighborhood with narrow lots, small gardens, two-bedroom houses, and trees to shade the sidewalks. On Sunday mornings the streets were peaceful and empty. Only chubby Eddy Emanoff would creak by on his old bike and, like some bemused Paul Revere, try to rouse the neighborhood to a ballgame at the schoolyard. Not a soul ever showed up before lunch. Eddy knew that, but he liked to creak about on that bike anyway, up the street and down the back lane, only to end up lying on our lawn trying to talk me into trading my Mickey Mantle card for some weird guy named Turk Lown.

After a Hungarian lunch of slow-simmered chicken soup, roast meats with paprika and sour cream sauce, a cucumber salad, and enough buttery, flakey, fresh-baked pastry to feed an army, I was out the door, my baseball glove in hand, running for the field with my mother shouting, "Be careful yourself! What happen if you die?"

Then we played ball. We had no teams, coaches, uniforms, or bases, only an old chipped bat and a few gloves that we shared, and the school yard was no well-manicured diamond but an old soccer field of gravel and dusty weeds. The gravel caused unexpected bounces in the gut and privates but you got used to that—what irked you was the short, right-field fence less than two hundred feet away. And Al Crowder. The bastard hit left-handed. Squinty little eyes, cigarette dangling from his mouth, and bang—a home run. John Hardy would climb the fence when Crowder came to bat, but bloody Crowder never hit right to him, so Hardy would end up talking to Mrs. Thompson working her vegetable garden in her floppy hat.

We picked teams by sticking our feet in a circle and someone reeling off "Engine, engine number nine going down Chicago line," after which we'd yell and fight over who got to play where. Then we'd settle down and play serious ball, quiet and concentrated, until Eddy Emanoff hit one of his hard grounders to the fence and rounded first base chuckling and puffing, but second base was a bit uphill and Eddy never made it because Jerry Allye would jump him, drag him down, and beat him with his glove while Eddy died laughing. Some of us would wander off during the game and others wander in; sometimes parents stopped by to watch and some even stayed to play, Ernie Flint running the bases in his worn-out slippers.

When the sun got so low it shone in our eyes, we went home. One day the fog rolled in and we snuck off and left Hardy sitting on the fence.

On hot summer Sundays our family went fishing. We would get in our old twenty-horsepower Austin built like a tank and also crawled like one—and we'd putt-putt out to a creek a half-hour from the house, grownups with kids, grownups without kids, kids without grown-ups, nobody really cared. It was a lousy place to fish. You might hook a few catfish or a carp, but the hayfields were a nice place to lie, or you could kick a ball around down on the bank. The willows gave you shade, and, in a bend, where the water was shallow, the mud on the bottom squished between your toes. Later, we'd build a fire and make a stew from everybody's fish in a big pot and drink lots of homemade wine and just lie around and talk. We seemed to talk a lot on all those Sundays.

But that was years ago.

The Mechanized Sunday

I visited friends in Florida last spring. Paradise. Palm trees, canals, bougainvilleas, gardenias, majestic white egrets standing in the shoals. I looked forward to sleeping in on Sunday morning but jumped awake to a sound like an F15 landing on the roof. It was a leaf blower. On the canal, jet skis screamed and cigarette boats roared. On the street, kids on motorbikes without mufflers leapt over curved ramps, and on the perfect lawns, mowers the size of our Austin, bore large, grumpy men crouched like warriors riding tanks to war. By ten, it was rush hour. Campers and SUVs stacked to the roof with gear driving to the beach, a ten-minute walk away. There was a bottleneck at the entrance to the mall. It hadn't yet opened but the parking lot was jammed. On Sunday, our day of rest.

I headed down to the beach on foot—not easy without sidewalks—using the road or people's front lawns, dodging cars and the menacing mowers. At the mall, I asked a man in the waiting crowd if there was a special sale. Nope, this was just an ordinary Sunday.

That afternoon I stopped to watch a kids' ballgame. My God, what a ballpark! A real diamond: a pitcher's mound, AstroTurf infield, raked sand between bases, real bases, dugouts, benches, uniforms, spikes, kids with their own gloves and kid-gloves for batting, and bats. Man, did they have bats, racks of aluminum bats. Enough to melt down and build yourself a 747.

And yet, awash in all that material splendor, everyone was as somber as soldiers going off to war. Anxious parents loudly urged victory, coaches kicked dirt, agitated kids yelled tired slogans, and, growing frustrated, threw their gloves in anger. The worst was when kids in the field came to bat. The coach hectored them to "stay aggressive, give 'em hell, get the hate up, go in for the kill!" because they had those guys "scared now," they had them "on the run."

What was this? War? Or just kids playing ball? Couldn't they wait until they grew up to have a bad time? Where was chubby Eddy? Or Ernie Flint in his worn-out slippers?

Maybe I'm raving; maybe the years are coloring my youth. But I don't think so. I remember a lot of bad, but not on Sundays.

You may rightly ask what on earth has a ballgame got to do with our besieged environment or endangered society. Well, it seems to me, everything. Not only was the ball game an environmental disaster, with the enormous quantity of energy consumed and pollution emitted to fabricate all those bats, uniforms, bleachers, and all, but what broke my heart, was that despite the gear, the material goods, there wasn't a kid out there having any fun. Sure they played well, snapped a throw, showed hustle, but where was the joy? The freedom? The laughter? Where was that burst of irrepressible urge that made Dave Dowset chase a fly ball deep and, after making the catch, keep running through the gate and vanish around a corner, leaving us all standing there without a ball, only to return from the fruit stand with a bag of cherries?

We shared those cherries just as we shared the gloves. That's why we came. Not just to hit home runs or beat the other guy—we played as hard as we could, we really tried—but there was more. We came to be together. To be friends.

It didn't matter whose team you played on, or who hit best or who caught best; it didn't matter how old you were, or if you were—God forbid—a girl, and it didn't even matter if you were fat and slow. It would have been unthinkable to play a game without Eddy; the day would have been sad without his laughter.

So we played together, and sat around together, and learned to get along without parents, without coaches, on our own. We learned how to make each other laugh, and what would make us cry, and learned that if something hurt one of us it would somehow hurt us all. And I learned that you can use the same scruffy ball and chipped bat for years and still be happy, that you can have as much fun in old sneakers as in spikes, and that all the new gear my mother would struggle to buy me could never be worth one of her Sunday meals.

CHAPTER 4

Love Thy Neighbor, Live Forever

*"Friendship is the only cement that
will ever hold the world together."*

—WOODROW WILSON

YOU MIGHT THINK that neighborly togetherness and its casual daily exchanges are good for a once-a-year laugh and no more. Well, there is empirical proof that a supportive community goes way beyond being fodder for sitcoms.

For decades I have pondered the immeasurable value of friends. I have talked in various books about those childhood days in Vancouver, surrounded by good pals, and later by our neighbors, the Paoluccis, in Montepulciano, who literally adopted us and brought us up as good Tuscans, leaving out those few but precious nearly lifelong friends just thinking of whom makes me confident and secure. And all along I have tried to describe the importance of small and daily friendships, the sense of sanctuary you feel in a small community, where you are known and appreciated, where you feel sheltered, where you belong.

But all along I could describe only vague feelings of calm and happiness, and a sense of well-being those relationships can bring. You can imagine what a confirmation of these hazy hunches and intuitions it was to find a piece of medical and sociological research which actually *quantified* the health benefits and long life that a reassuring and nurturing community could provide.

A friend in New York who knew I was working on this book sent me an excerpt from the respected and bestselling writer Malcolm Gladwell and thought it would help. It was a chapter from his intriguing book *Outliers*. Not only did it help me in writing this, but it also convinced me that I hadn't lost my mind.

Gladwell cites research done almost 50 years ago by Stewart Wolf, a physician who taught in the medical school at the University of Oklahoma but spent his summer months on a farm in Pennsylvania.

Near Wolf's farm was the small Italian immigrant town of Roseto where, one day, he stumbled onto something his sociologist and co-researcher John Bruhn later called "magical."

Roseto, Pennsylvania was named after Roseto, Italy a small medieval hill town in the rugged landscape of the southern region of Puglia, whose inhabitants eked out a living from a marble quarry and the terraced hillsides near the town. In 1882, in search of a better life, twelve of them sailed to America and found jobs in a slate quarry of eastern Pennsylvania.

Following their success, Rosetans began to emigrate en mass. In 1894 alone, 1,200 of them applied for passports. On a rocky hillside of Pennsylvania, they began to build a town that very much resembled the one they had left behind; in the town square they built a church they named after the one in Puglia, on the narrow streets they built closely-packed, two—story houses with slate roofs, and, their main street they named after Italy's national hero, Garibaldi.

In the last years of the century, an energetic young priest Don De Nisco gave a vibrant life to the new town. Gladwell writes, "De Nisco set up spiritual societies and organized festivals. He encouraged the townsfolk to clear the land, and plant onions, beans, potatoes, melons and fruit trees in the long backyards behind their houses. He gave out seeds and bulbs. The town came to life."

When Wolf arrived more than fifty years later, he found a perfect social replica of an Italian town that his co-researcher Bruhn later described. "I remember going

to Roseto for the first time, and you'd see three genera-
tional family meals, all the bakeries, the people walking
up and down the street, sitting on their porches talking
to each other...It was magical."

But the true magic lay in the health of the people of
Roseto. The local doctor who had been practicing there
for seventeen years told Wolf, "'I rarely find anyone from
Roseto under the age of sixty-five with heart disease."

This was back in the 1950s, long before broad knowledge
of cholesterol when, "Heart attacks were an epidemic in
the United States." Wolf was skeptical but smitten. With
the help of the local mayor who put not only the town's
council room at Wolf's disposal but also the help of his four
sisters, Wolf began to analyze physicians' records recon-
structing medical histories and family genealogies. He
invited the whole town to be tested, blood samples, EKG's,
the works. They found the results astonishing. In Roseto,
virtually no one under the age of fifty-five showed any
signs of heart disease. For men over sixty-five, the death
rate from heart disease was roughly half that of the US
average. The death rate from *all* causes was about a third
lower than it should have been. Bruhn recalls, "There
was no suicide, no alcoholism, no drug addiction, and very
little crime. They didn't have anyone on welfare. Then
we looked at peptic ulcers. They didn't have any of those
either. These people were dying of old age. That's it."

The question of course was "Why?"

The hunt was on.

The first suspect was diet. They thought that their Mediterranean cuisine brought over from Puglia, high in olive oil, seafood, vegetables and fruit, might have caused them to be healthier than their fellow Americans. But that wasn't true: the Rosetans no longer cooked with olive oil but used lard instead, their pizzas were heavy and besieged by salami, sausage, ham and even eggs: over 40 percent of their calories came from fat. They also smoked heavily. So much for health habits.

THEY NEXT TRIED genetics. They traced down relatives of Rosetans in other parts of America to see if their good health matched. No go: Rosetan good health did not go past the boundaries of the town.

Next, they wondered if it was the Pennsylvanian hills that made the difference. Two nearby, same-sized towns, Bangor and Nazareth, were populated by similarly hardworking European immigrants. They scoured the medical records: for men over 65, the death rates from heart disease were three times that of Roseto.

After years of research, Wolf and Bruhn, stumbled on the answer to what made Rosetans healthy: it was Roseto; their town.

Gladwell eloquently concludes: "They looked at how the Rosetans visited each other, stopping to chat with each other in Italian on the street, or cooking for each other in their backyards. They learned about the extended family clans that underlay the town's social structure. They saw how many homes had three generations living under one roof, and how much respect grandparents commanded. They went to Mass at Our Lady of Mt. Carmel Church and saw the unifying and calming effect of the church. They counted twenty-two separate civic organizations in a town of just under 2,000 people. They picked up on the particular egalitarian ethos of the town, that discouraged the wealthy from flaunting their success and helped the unsuccessful obscure their failures.

"In transplanting the *paesani culture* of southern Italy to the hills of eastern Pennsylvania the Rosetans had created a powerful, protective social structure capable of insulating them from the pressures of the modern world. The Rosetans were healthy because of where they were *from*, because of the world they had created for themselves in their tiny little town in the hills."

So whatever you do, and however you do it, you should make a concentrated effort to forever love thy neighbor, and not because the Bible tells you so, but because it can lead to a longer and *much* healthier life.

PERHAPS EPICURUS, THE Athenian philosopher who died in 270 BC, was right when he wrote, "It's not so much our friend's help that helps us, as the confident knowledge that he *will* help us."

CHAPTER 5

A Man's Neighborhood
is His Castle

OF COURSE YOU'LL have by now shut the book and
heaved it in exasperation across the room, grumbling
"What the hell does he want us to do? Suddenly become
Italians, move to Pennsylvania, start digging a town into
the hillside and grow our own food and make our own
pasta?"

Not quite. But there is nothing to keep you, whether
you live in a city or a sprawling impersonal suburb, from
reorganizing into small, healthy, livable, loveable, ener-
gizing, socially and emotionally rewarding Rosetos. It
might take getting to know your neighbors and changing a few bylaws, but those are in a desperate need of
change anyway. The resultant new communities will not
only bring long life and good health but also provide the
security and happiness that a life *without* "suicide, alcoholism, drug addiction, and crime," can assure.

. . .

A MIRACULOUSLY SUCCESSFUL instant village was born in North America just thirty years ago. When I lived there it was a remote rugged valley of a few hundred houses, scattered helter-skelter over a five-mile stretch. It had a pub, two small hotels, a school, a big muddy parking lot, and a gas station that doubled as a grocery store. Applications came in to build a giant supermarket at one end, a building supply store at the other, and a café and bar at another spot, but the town's councilmen, in typically hesitant Canadian fashion, held off and, for years, talked about building a village center. It was finally decided that the best spot was a bench-land near the school and asked the owner—the federal government—to sell it to the town. The government obliged. It was the local dump.

Next a citizen committee was formed, along with potential would-be local investors to decide what shape the new village should take. The committee traveled the world to get ideas. They settled on a center built around a pedestrian town square. There were to be 25 small buildings with commercial space on the ground floor and two storeys residential above. Only town residents could develop each site, and each developer was limited to one parcel. So the local pub owner took one, as did the local carpenter. The town center was built in a year. The shops and residences filled instantly; the new town was full of life night and day. It has since more than tripled in size, but remained pedestrian.

Skeptics would ask, "But how can a place like that turn a profit?"

Well, I bought a lot in a hillside in 1977 then sold it a couple of years later when we moved on. Since that time, real estate prices in New York City quintupled; that lot sold this spring for *thirty-six times* its 1977 price.

Meanwhile, the town has won awards for Excellence in Energy Conservation, Clean Energy, Excellence in Environmental Education, and Excellence in Stakeholder Relations. Last year the town hosted the Winter Olympics. Its name is Whistler, BC.

Because the people who lived there wanted a beautiful, humane town, they managed to convert a muddy garbage dump into one of the most sought after places to live.

TO START REMAKING our cities and suburbs into true neighborhoods, we will have to overcome two ludicrous notions.

The first is that "bigger is better." It's not; it's awful. There is no comparison between walking through an enormous parking lot, buying a loaf of plastic-wrapped bread in a humongous supermarket and paying for it at a cashier who can't be bothered to look you in the eye (who can blame him), and strolling down Garibaldi Avenue stopping every few steps to greet a neighbor, shop owner or friend—or someone you absolutely recognize but have no clue from where—and exchanging a few pleasantries before you make it to Muriel the baker, and wait in line with people you know, while inhaling the magic fragrance of fresh bread and pastry, and then chatting with Muriel about what loaves she has left: some nice seven-grain or wood-fire baked peasant bread and how much handmade pasta should you buy for tonight because there are six of you for dinner, a neighbor (eats like a horse), plus a cousin (what a bore) and a good friend. And what about some wonderful dessert? What has she got that's really creamy, chocolaty and disgustingly gooey?

I think you'll all agree the first example is bare survival, the second is *real life*.

"A MAN'S HOME is his castle?" A man's home is *much* larger than his castle. His *home* includes not only his yard but his neighborhood, and the town square or main street where he takes his evening stroll with the whole town every night; it includes his neighbors and his friends and the butcher and the baker and the post-mistress and the kids who always tip over his garbage can. They all contribute much more than the four walls—the walls and roof just keep out the rain, but his friends and neighbors feed his soul and make him think, make him laugh, and make him care about others and the world. No matter how you arm your walls with security devices, insurance riders and electronic gear, none of that will give you the physical or emotional security of caring friends and neighbors, and none of it will ever replace a single brief encounter that might enrich your life and stay a sweet memory for a long time.

Stick *that* in your Hallmark card.

Why love Thy Neighbor

Just how far our society has drifted from real life and real friends is chillingly summarized in a letter from a Mr. Rivers reprinted in a recent piece from *The Milford Daily News*. He writes, "Many of my best friends today don't even know me at all. They would include Pamela Anderson on "Dancing with the Stars," Vanna White and Pat Sajak on "Wheel of Fortune," Meredith Vieira on "Who Wants To Be A Millionaire" and John O'Hurley, host of "Family Feud." Little do they know that I look forward to seeing each of them several times a week, even if I can't spell their names. Friends are out there and we all should have lots of them!"

On first blush I thought, oh yes. On second, I was horrified. I envisioned Mr. Rivers staring at the tube, saying nothing, feeling close to nothing, living alone, dying alone, and days passing before someone gets a whiff that he is dead.

It is little wonder then that we slowly lose our minds

when we add to Mr. River's list of "best friends" Rush Limbaugh and Glenn Beck who rant at us incoherently. But then how would we know that it's all bullshit on wings? We have no real friends to shake us, and tell us that Rush and Glenn are *not* our friends, they don't care what idiocy they utter, nor could they care whether you live or die as long as you buy the product of their sponsor.

I mean if you stood in line at Muriel's awaiting your still warm strawberry rhubarb pie, and told your neighbors around you that you thought the proposed Park 51 in lower Manhattan will bring "thousands and thousands" of Muslims into the area and "the next thing you know they'll take over city council and pass an ordinance that calls for public prayer five times a day," one of two things would happen: everyone might guffaw and declare what a wonderfully creative comic you are, *or* they would rush you outside to get some oxygen to your brain before it's too late.

But if Pat Robertson says it on his "700 club" (as he did word for word) then it becomes a messianic warning with which the populace rises up in arms. And Mr. Rivers gently nods and thanks his good friend Pat for the early warning. As Timothy Egan wrote in *The New York Times*, ". . . these people bemoan, detest and feign outrage over utter fantasies."

And isolated people like Mr. Rivers can't help but believe them.

Where on Earth was I? Oh yes, a man's castle.

Now you might say that Roseto and small towns are a quaint Italian thing, that the rest of the world has moved on and we do just fine with virtual neighbors and electronic friends. But I disagree. The same human longing that binds together the people of Roseto, echoes around the world as far away and in as different a culture as that of Beijing, China.

An ancient Beijing neighborhood called Gulou, 32 charmingly decrepit acres, is about to be torn down and turned into a flashy tourist attraction to be meaninglessly named Beijing Time Cultural City. One of the residents bitterly opposed is 55 year old Mr. Liu, a martial arts master, gruff and tough, who says he has no interest in being given a new steel and concrete apartment in exchange for his humble home. "It's a treasure to live in a place where you know the people and where your family has lived for generations," said Mr. Liu, who shares his home with three others, including his 81-year-old father. "Who wants to live in a place where you can live next door to someone and not talk to them for years?"

Amen to that, Brother Liu.

So what to do?

Once we accept the above truths that bigger is not better, and that your whole community is home, the rest will just take some bureaucratic wrangling, a bit of elbow grease, some imagination, and a few belly laughs.

The suburbs are a cakewalk. There has never been a better time than now for do-it-yourself urban replanning. When a good percentage of homes in many neighborhoods are foreclosed or abandoned, and 15 million people are out of work, would it not make sense to rezone our sprawling 'burbs—where there isn't a school or a park or a store within miles—turning lifeless neighborhoods into lively villages with schools, parks, greenspace and small shops, full of life day and night? I'm sure you'll recoil and say "what would this village look like?" The first thing to decide is size. Villagers should be able to get everywhere *on foot*. This is easy as pie. If each village was about a quarter of a square mile (that's 160 acres with 8 lots per acre) we end up with about 1,000 houses allotting for roads making the very longest about 500 yards ie five football fields which even a rheumatic snail can manage. A thousand houses would yield on average about 3,000 people; the perfect Roseto.

Now, with a bit of creativity and a bit of scrambling we can easily remodel each newly divided unit into a friendly little town.

First of all, the town square is a must for that is where you'll—besides doing a bit of shopping—meet your friends and neighbors, have a beer, glass of wine or cappuccino and discuss how to run the world; your world, the one that is your castle, your hometown. Around this small square which needs to be no bigger than the average suburban lot, you can rezone the houses into residential *and* commercial, the commercial parts being a few shops the new village desperately needs: a butcher, a baker, a fruit and vegetable store, a daycare center, a bar, a café, a bookstore, and a nice family-owned and run restaurant, and of course that long lost treasure: the general store which has a bit of hardware, a bit of this and a bit of everything.

The one stipulation has to be *no* chain stores, no fast food and no junk food sales, thank you. Let each storeowner decide what is best for the *health* of the village, and let each of them fulfill these needs his or her own way (more about this later). It is a given that more and more people will dig up their lawns to plant vegetables and fruit trees. The local store would be an excellent outlet for these and whatever jams, preserves, pies the village cold turn out. Since these stores need not be large, the size of an average double garage will more than nicely do—in our medieval hill town of Montalcino, the average store is 300 square feet. The shop-owners can live as before in the house itself, avoiding commuting and extra expense. They would never get rich serving 3,000 people but they'd have the enormous satisfaction of not only being their own bosses and making a decent living, but also have the pride of contributing to the well-being of their town.

• • •

OUR WHOLE SOCIETY could change if we stopped being slaves to the car. We could for starters diminish its importance by closing off most suburban streets, and parking the rusting beasts in a common parking lot located at each corner. Yes, you'd have to walk a few steps to your house. Our car is 200 feet from our front door and it's actually nice to walk past trees and through the garden before you're indoors again.

This would have an infinite number of social and economic benefits. First, half our streets could become green again, forming great spaces where children can play, teenagers gather, and neighbors gossip and set the whole world right.

Crime will be decimated because break-ins and get-aways would be much more difficult, so kids could be safely shoved out the front door in the morning and told not to set foot in the house before lunch.

Next, our massive garages could become fruitful spaces, anything from offices to small craft studios to huge greenhouses (all you have to do is put skylights in the roof), where a family could grow food in any season, including lemons and oranges in Fargo, North Dakota, but more on this on the chapter The Food Garden.

With all this inviting open green space even the worst couch potato or videogame addict would be tempted out-doors for some fresh air and an unforgettable game of touch-football. Or he could just hang out, walk the dog, gossip, or have an impromptu cookout on the common barbecue; all more healthy and emotionally rewarding activities than sitting inside, alone, staring at flickering lights, growing cellulite.

Some such new "green" communities are even more creative. They dig ponds not only adding fishing and row boating fun for their children, but, by bringing in varied wildlife, giving children a chance to get to know the beauty and mystery of nature.

I'm sure you can envision the vibrancy and vivacity of such a community, easily achievable given some goodwill.

WHERE DO WE start? In Britain, the Department for Communities and Local Government announced a competition to build up to 10 eco-towns. To give us an idea what to aim for environmentally, it might be instructive to see what standards eco-towns were required to meet.

1. Eco-towns must be zero-carbon over the course of a year (not including transport emissions).
2. A minimum of 40 percent of eco-towns must be green space. (This is a snap if you close half the roads).
3. At least one job opportunity per house must be accessible by public transport, walking or cycling.
4. There must be shops and a primary school within easy walk of every home.

5. A public transport link must be within a ten minute walk of every home.

6. There must be a mixture of housing types and densities, and residents must have a say in how their town is run, by governance in new and innovative ways.

The idea of self-governed and even self-sufficient villages is not a new invention. It has been advocated by such profound humanists as Tolstoy and Gandhi, both of whom thought that it would leave each individual not only with the best physical and emotional support, but would allow him the greatest democratic participation in society and furnish him with the most freedom.

Gandhi saw our political system as a huge power structure with each layer of government having an increasing level of authority over the one below it. He wanted the opposite: a society in which nothing was done without the consent of the individual.

His idea was that true self-rule in a country means that every person rules himself or herself, and that there is no state which enforces laws upon the people. Rather, people are self-governed by mutual responsibilities. When Gandhi received a letter asking for his participation in writing a world charter for human rights, he responded saying, "In my experience, it is far more important to have a charter for human duties."

It seems the people of Roseto have developed—without writing a charter—just like that.

The idea of self-rule of course never caught on because if we all lived as Gandhi thought we should—responsible, honorable, with the health and welfare of our fellow villagers in mind—there would never be a place for the current legion of bought politicians, or robber barons, or CEO's who make a million bucks a day, or raving media half-wits. And the boys of Wall Street could then take their mortgage-backed-securities-and-collateralized-debt-obligations and . . . Exactly.

OK, I might be raving, but you can feel in your gut that I'm right.

To rezone and remodel our lives into authentic neighborhoods would take mostly goodwill and some work by every neighbor. There would be costs incurred but if we can find $700 billion to bail out millionaires, and $1 trillion *a year* for the military (no, that's no typo and that sum does not include the approximately $100 billion for the CIA) to fight supposed enemies, then I'm sure a few thousand per family can be found to get new villages started—safe, healthy, vibrant, free of crime—villages that could serve the whole world as a shining example, the sturdy new foundation it so desperately needs.

The New Cities

For years, when in Manhattan, I stayed near Gramercy Park: midtown. It was an area of high-rise apartment

buildings, equally tall offices, vast impersonal supermarkets, and restaurants the size of a nice gymnasium. Last
year I changed digs and moved to Greenwich Village. I
felt as if I had come to New York for the first time. The
buildings were small, the apartments in them miniscule
(mine was 300 feet). The restaurants, bars and cafes
friendly, cozy, and the shops, my God, it was like coming
home.

The narrow streets here are lined with trees, small
parks, and street benches are everywhere, and there's
Washington Square with its circus atmosphere, and
Union Square with its Farmer's Market. Near me, in a
nook, an Italian food store close to a hundred years old
sells homemade pasta, homemade sauces, and preserves.
Down the street a tiny milk and cheese store makes
fresh mozzarella twice a week. Close by is a baker with
mountains of fresh bread and pastries, a block away is a
Greek restaurant with only five tables, across the street
a Cuban one with eight. You can walk from one end of
the village to the other in ten minutes, and if you can't
find what you need in one of its hundred small shops, it
probably doesn't exist. At night there are innumerable
bars, off-Broadway theaters, comedy clubs, and performance spaces, dives and lounges, and streets so bristling
with life that even the dead-have been known to get up
and boogie.

If you know a place in the world with a more vibrant,

more varied, and more creative people, please, I beg
you, send me its address. Village people are as open and
friendly as you can ask for. My apartment building has
ten small suites. Within the first week, I knew half the
tenants. In midtown, after twenty years, out of about
two hundred, I knew only two. The obvious objection
will be, "Yes, but it's a very expensive part of town." It
is expensive because people seek that "village feeling",
even though it means living in phone booth-sized apartments with steep five-floor walkups. But the same can
be felt in parts of Brooklyn or Queens for much less, and
can easily be recreated in any major city.

So there is our model for the ideal city: Greenwich
Village. We need not imagine or invent anything, all we
need to do is copy what is there and even improve on it,
first by getting rid of cars. Believe me it can be done; if
it works in Venice, with only one main canal for public
transport, there is no reason it can't work in Manhattan
or anywhere else where criss-crossing streets abound.

As every Venetian or visitor to Venice will tell you:
there is no city on earth that makes you feel so proud.
I don't mean because of the architecture or the *campi*
or the twisting narrow *rios*; I mean pride from sensing
that the city was built with only one thing in mind: its
people, and their daily and eternal enjoyment in being
human.

CHAPTER 6

The True Cost of a Thing

BEFORE WE MAKE major changes to our cities and suburbs, we need to know not only what to do, but what to avoid.

The best way to ascertain both is to step back and evaluate what Thoreau called "the true cost of a thing." What he meant was not only the monetary value of an object; that was too simple, it missed the whole point. The "true cost" is what that object costs as a portion of one's life or, indeed, what the cost is to society as a whole.

Look for a moment at where we have arrived and what it cost us to get here.

FOR MUCH OF our existence as a species, we lived in a true garden. We were sometimes cold, sometimes sweltering in the sun, but our air was clean, the valleys lush and endless, and the soil we tilled was pure, the seas we fished were crystal clear, and the beaches where we gathered shellfish were as pristine as on the day of their creation. We drank the water of a spring with joy and confidence. And our lives were full of mystery and wonder like the moon that climbed the sky a different shape each night and could drive men mad and even raise the seas.

We felt a constant closeness to nature then. We prayed to the sky for rain, prayed to the soil for sustenance; we knew the name of every tree and plant, the dozens of different cloud formations, how animals ran, where they slept, and how they held their heads when a storm was on its way. We were at home in the world. It is true that we were superstitious and fearful, frightened by beasts, eclipses, ghosts and thunder, but we had magic, and dances to drive our dreads away. Our lives might have been short—thirty to forty years—but the intensity of daily survival made them seem much longer.

With the exception of a few cities that rose to great heights then fell—Rome went from nearly three million inhabitants at its apex to barely fifty-thousand at its fall—we lived in villages and towns and worked mostly at home, for ourselves. We grew or raised our own food; our houses were built with the help of our friends, and what else we needed—our tools and clothes—were made by craftsmen of the village, the weaver, the cobbler, the smithy—and were made to last a lifetime. What small scars we left on the land, soon healed. We lived at a slow pace and most often died in the place where we were born.

The Industrial Revolution of the eighteenth century, considered by historians as *the* great event in human history, indisputably not only sped up but vastly enriched our lives. Trains, ships, canals, and railroads shortened trips from months to days; what had required a weaver weeks to produce by hand, a machine could do in minutes.

But industry and commerce also massed us in the cities, giving rise to broken communities, social isolation and to diseases incubated and spread by overcrowding, like cholera and tuberculosis—the latter is on a new rampage in India where their Industrial Revolution is barely underway.

London's population of one hundred thousand in the seventeenth century soared to seven million by the end of the eighteen-hundreds.

The Technological Revolution of the early nineteen-hundreds brought us more to celebrate: the airplane, the automobile, refrigeration, the telephone, and perhaps most vital of all, the mass production of consumer goods.

Urbanization saw its Golden Age. Vienna, Paris, London and New York became marvels of boulevards, sprawling parks, and dazzling architecture dotted with universities, museums, libraries and opera houses. We became better educated, lived longer, had unlimited choices of careers, places to live, things to buy and had millions of neighbors, although we might not have known any.

Then came the digital age. The world and everyone in it lay suddenly at our fingertips.

We have progressed beyond our wildest dreams.

But at what cost?

What besides our independence and self-reliance did we—most often unwittingly—relinquish in exchange? What was the effect all these goods and gizmos had on our health, both physical and mental? And how do they bode for our long-term economy, our environment and, perhaps most importantly, our social selves?

The cost to our economy—after depressions, bubbles and recessions—is easy to enumerate, the environment likewise, but how does one measure the cost to the most precious things of all: the happiness of our children, the loyalty of our friends, even our love and joy? And how far did each leap forward in our "standard of living," separate us from our neighbors, our close-knit community, our dear, life-long friendships, and even from ourselves? How much did we lose of our spontaneous, passionate, and compassionate humanness?

We were told that mechanization would free us from labor and shower us with leisure time. It didn't. Then we were told that hi-tech breakthroughs would certainly do the same; yet we're more frantic and hurried than ever before. Is it not possible that what America's celebrated philosopher Lewis Mumford called our "mad senseless, unthinking, commitment to technological change we call progress," has battered not only our economy and our planet but also *us*? For are we really any more secure, happy or healthy today, having changed from the relatively stable, self-reliant, sociable small town folks we were for millennia, to the breathtakingly competitive, super stressed, yet arguably more lonely city dwellers of today?

And what now, now that our basic needs for security, love, friendship and fulfillment have come to take a back seat to things of fictitious importance: fame, wealth, and the short-term profit needs of enormous corporations, whose obsession with expansion and growth has come to dictate how we live each day?

The answer to these questions lies beyond spreadsheets and numbers; it lies—if you'll excuse the simplistic and sentimental—in our guts and hearts.

So perhaps it's easiest to begin by examining something tangible: our economy.

The Economic Cost

> "Given the tumult of the past few years,
> the barter system is starting to look good."
>
> —JAMES SUROWIECKI, *The New Yorker*

Until not long ago, the barter system *was* good. I made a pair of shoes and wanted to eat roast piglet; you had piglets and needed shoes so we'd cut a deal. How big a piglet for how good a shoe depended on how hungry I was and how sick you were of walking in bare feet. The conditions were reassuringly simple: we both *saw* exactly what we were getting, and we both had to be happy with the results. Since we knew each other in the community, the likelihood of one of us cheating the other was low, not only for fear of public objection but also because I would surely find you and club you on the head.

Once currency was introduced, we began to lose control. Not only was the value of our money open to interpretation and inflation—but, more importantly, it was easy to forget just *how much* of our lives, how much work, we expended for those coins; an occurrence much less likely with the piglet. So not only were we at the mercy of outside forces, but we were, even more so, victims of our own spotty memory. We began to spend.

The more goods the Industrial Revolution and world trade laid at our feet, the more dazzled we became and the more we shopped. And the more depressed we became in overcrowded cities, working most often in unfulfilling jobs, the more we shopped to forget our misery.

The more we shopped, the richer a tiny fragment of society—owners of factories, banks and trading companies—became. Their unused money, or surplus profit, was gathering dust so they began to invest. Enormous projects like railroads and canals were built, rarely to improve people's lives, but, rather, to make unused money grow.

And grow it did. In 1830 there were but "a few dozen miles" of railway in the world, but by 1850 there were 23,000. Since then "progress" has basically run amok. We raised dams, paved valleys, (every year the US paves

1.3 million acres of formerly unpaved land, almost *twice* the size of the Hawaiian Islands) we strip-mined, clear-cut, tunneled, bridged, under-passed and over-passed.

We drained lakes and marshlands, built indoor ski slopes in the Dubai desert, heated our driveways and cooled our beaches, all with piles of money that some one wanted to make even larger.

When we saw how much money was to be made through investment, we the common folk, helped by programs like 401K's, invested our hard-earned cash. We seldom knew or cared where our money went as long as there was more of it when it finally returned.

When we ran out of concrete things to invest in, the financial wizards invented abstract things like Structured Investment Vehicles, Credit Default Swaps and Collateralized Debt Obligations, which no one completely understood and made snake oil sound legitimate. Yet the fundamental problem with these financial innovations was not only that they left investors in the dark, but, propelled by unscrupulous salesmen and computer programmed buying and selling, which overwhelmed and excluded slow human response, investors and even executives forgot to think for themselves.

BESIDES BLIND MASS-INVESTMENT, which led us to the brink, there was another wonderful invention: mass credit.

As recently as the 1930s, most middle and working

class people had no major debt. This was in part due to common sense and prudence, and, in part, because banks were hesitant to lend to them. Most people rented their homes, or if they owned a house, it had been paid for bit-by-bit as it was being built. Mortgages—which when paid off cost on average more than twice the original price—were few and far between.

After the war, with government-backed loans, mortgages bloomed. They were seen as an investment because the value of our homes kept rising as both the population—hence the demand for houses—and our real income, slowly but steadily grew. This dependable rise took place thanks to prudent bankers, who gave mortgages to those with proven credit, steady income, and a sizable down payment—"prime" customers, who were pretty likely to pay back a loan.

But around the year 2000, our bankers unexpectedly put common sense aside. When they ran out of "primes" to lend to, they lunged after "sub-primes:" people with no steady job, no credit, and no funds for a down payment. With this newly invented market, house prices went sky high. Everyone was buying, looking for a quick-flip profit. One Florida secretary with an annual income of $20,000 bought herself three $400,000 houses in a week. The thinking—if there was any—was that if the sub-primer defaulted on his mortgage, he could simply sell, pay off the mortgage and with house prices infinitely rising, pocket a tidy profit. But the question no one answered, or worse, no one asked, was, "Sell the house to *whom?*" Since the people who could afford houses, the "primes," had houses, as now did all of those who really couldn't afford them, the "sub-primes," who could next be dredged up and convinced to buy? Who in the populace was even more jobless, credit-less, savings less? The homeless? Pre-schoolers? The unborn?

Just asking.

So the housing bubble, like the stock market bubble of '87 and the tech bubble of '02, burst in '08 and we now have a quarter of American mortgage holders under water (their mortgage is more than their house is worth); 40 percent of homes in Florida and a whopping 70 percent of those in Nevada.

When the housing bubble burst, house prices crashed, taking banks and the stock market with it. Tens of millions lost the equity (their life savings) in their homes, millions actually lost their homes, many more millions saw their private investment pension plans wiped out, but worst: the crash took with it modestly living people who had never gone near an investment in their lives, who were among the eight million who lost their job that year.

IF THE MORTGAGE fiasco didn't quite bury us, there was yet another device to squeeze out last drops of blood: the credit card.

At first blush the credit card seems like seventh heaven: you have no money so you simply utter, "charge." But, in fact, the credit card has been one of the most success-ful weapons to defeat reality and propel us into a life of illusion.

While in the 1930s people lived debt free—in fact, having debt was seen as a moral failure—by 2009 the average household debt—not counting mortgage debt—was $14,500. You shrug and say, So what, but consider that a typical credit card purchase ends up costing 112 percent *more* than if cash were used, and the fact that almost half of American families spend more than they earn, you can readily see how we are being sucked into a whirl-pool of debt.

What we pay over-all is shown by the fact that the credit-card industry, charging an average of 19% inter-est, took in $43 billion last year just in fees.

Nothing wrong with credit cards you say if you use them wisely, true but wisdom seems to be a seldom deployed tool. A revealing statistic demonstrates the mental distance between reality and fiction. In fast food restaurants people using credit cards spend up to 50% more than those who pay with cash. Now we can safely assume that the level of hunger in a populace is more or less the same, so it's telling that those who use *real* money, spend half as much as those who use plastic.

While 90 percent of Americans claim their credit card

debt has never been a source of worry, 50 percent refuse to tell a friend how much they really owe. It is as if they live in a virtual world, where, if you don't talk about it, debt doesn't exist. And since 60 percent of active card accounts are not paid off monthly, you have to wonder how many of us end up paying $4 for a $2 hamburger.

The cost of considerable progress in economic terms was twofold; first, we lost our security and self-reliance by moving to the city and working for others, subject to dismissal at the market's or boss's whim, but worse, we gradually removed ourselves from reality and began to live in a world of debt and dreams. When and how our bills would be paid seemed to interest almost no one, much as the day of reckoning was irrelevant to Bernie Madoff.

Until it came.

The Social Costs

I could write volumes about the social devastation that inventions such as the automobile have brought upon us; from creating endless commutes to the destruction of small towns, to the obliteration of peaceful neighborhoods by overpasses, clover-leaf intersections and freeways, but Henry Ford's curse on humanity is so universally beloved, despite global warming and mega oil spills, that we might as well just take a deep breath and move on to examine the social costs of more recent inventions.

Where the car gave us physical mobility, our new loves: the iPhone, the laptop, and Blackberry put us verbally in touch with the whole world. They allow us to have hundreds of friends, to send instant messages to one at a time or all at once, and share with them every moment of our lives. The problem is when we stop and admit to ourselves that, "I'm going to get an ice cream cone now," posted on your Facebook wall to be followed an hour later by, "My tummy hurts," are neither world shaking news events nor add one iota of strength to human bonds. They are neither informative nor funny (not intentionally anyway); what they are, indisputably, is a waste of time.

I don't mean to be the bearer of bad news, but we have only one life. Do we really want to spend precious moments of that miraculous event blasting banalities to people we never met and who, frankly my dear, couldn't give a damn?

I'm not going to dispute that cell phones can save lives: locate people lost in avalanches or at sea or in the garden gnome section of Home Depot, but they have somehow created an obsessive need to be *in touch* so much so that even a Benedictine monk interrupts his meditative evening walk on the cypress-bordered grounds of a monastery near us to feverishly text, "Don't forget the milk!"

A major proportion of this "social interaction" is no interaction at all. It's background noise. It resembles the soothing music of shopping malls which lulls you into zombie-like serenity that lets you shop until you drop.

With our communication machines constantly "on," even those precious moments of reflective solitude, or once in a lifetime romantic interludes with him on one knee asking you to be forever his wife are suddenly interrupted by the Thong Song or a marrow-shaking vibration near the groin.

Too often our messages are just electronic yawns: we're, like, *so* bored, so we click. Whose special moment we might be interrupting doesn't cross our minds.

What the constant contact mostly does is water down our lives. It drains the intensity out of emotions that may otherwise build to a passionate crescendo. It dissolves the expectation out of meeting a long lost lover; will she come, won't she come, what if she forgot me, what if she went and died? None of those thoughts can cross your mind when your little screen informs you that she just stepped off the subway; that now she's moving up the stairs; now she's turning right; and now she's stuck, OMG, at a traffic light.

And perhaps worst of all, instant communication gets us so involved in the lives of distant others, that we forget the people who really need us, our family and close friends. Just as the creation of freeways that enabled us to escape the cities led to their abandonment and demise, so the communication highway lets us take refuge in the undemanding relationship of some distant "friend," leaving the real ones behind.

Talk More, Feel Less

It might be worthwhile to look at the diminishing intensity of personal communication through the years. There is certainly no more passionate or rewarding an interaction than the physical face to face. Far beyond words exchanged, are emotional bonds reinforced by a glance, a smile, a touch: moments that might stay with us and nurture us for life.

We seem to have an innate need to see the impact of our words and this appears to be true even among those who spend ample time together.

Bridget and I worked on this book at adjoining desks, in easy hearing range. Yet when we wanted to talk, even to exchange a simple idea, we tended to turn and look in each other's eyes; there seemed to be a need to *completely communicate*. When I read this sentence to her she turned to me, "That's true," she said, and beamed a smile.

WHILE THE OLD-FASHIONED land phone lacked the physical exchange at least we usually sat down in a quiet place to make a call, concentrating our attention on what we heard and said. We could even close our eyes and be really thoughtful. Intonations and nuances fleshed out mere words. With the advent of the cell phone, most of that was lost. We call from anywhere with background noise aplenty; and we talk while we walk, drive, work, shop, barely listening, often distracted from what we say or hear. The nuances of tone are lost, not only because of the noise, but because we are often shouting to be heard. I cannot enumerate the number of frustrating shouting matches I terminated with, "I'll call you from my land phone so we can talk."

E-mail and texting, while potentially restoring time for thoughtfulness, have, because of their hurried nature, led to countless misunderstandings.

And while we still value voice contact and even more so the physical, our ever-growing tendency toward "social networking" erodes our need for the clutchable, huggable, other.

A Pew report issued in November 2009 and entitled "Social Isolation and New Technology" found that "users of social networking services are 26 percent less likely to use their neighbors as a source of companionship."

You might ask what is wrong with replacing time-consuming physical encounters with a myriad of less rewarding electronic ones? The answer is "nothing," if you're willing to admit that it's rather akin to giving up periodic but passionate, bone-crushing, lose-your-mind love-making for an endless game of tag.

Perhaps this whole phenomenon can be understood

considering our obsession with numbers. We seem to believe the more people know we exist and the more we are approved of in a virtual world, the more we exist. One of the most baffling phrases I heard someone utter was years ago when Madonna blurted "I want the whole world to know my name." Why? Or, as Bridget asked yesterday, "What good is it having a thousand Facebook friends when you have no one to talk to?"

A shocking story was that of Simone Back of Brighton, England. Her Facebook friends numbered over a thousand. On Christmas Day she posted that she was committing suicide. The police found her dead seventeen hours later. Not one of the thousand friends had come to her aid.

Loss of Time, Loss of Mind

How the slew of our communication gadgets has affected us, is best summed up by the following three quotes. The first is by Gerald Celente, the editor of *The Trends Journal*.

> Technology is supposed to free us from shackles of work and give us more leisure time. But it has proven the opposite. A 2005 Leger Marketing survey found that the majority of people feel technology has meant more work and less time with their family. Whether it's cell

phones, Blackberry's, video-games or e-mail, we have become a culture enslaved by electronics.

Humans are being trapped in a high-tech cycle that is freezing their minds away from the moment, looking at life and taking in what's around them. While technology has radically altered the externals of life, it has done nothing to enhance the internals: moral, emotional, philosophical and spiritual values.

And as Eric Slate wrote in *Adbuster* Magazine, "As people fall further into their personal gadgets, scientists and psychologists are now beginning to classify technology dependency as a major health problem, putting it in the same categories as alcoholism, gambling and drug addiction. The stress it creates is causing arthritis, migraines, and ulcers. But most troubling, it is having a powerful impact on our personal development. It seems the more 'connected' we are, the more detached we become."

The ultimate irony in an age in which we—and especially the techno-savvy young—constantly "communicate" is that we are losing the ability to speak. The following quote is from jobweb.org, a site that offers career and job-search advice for new college graduates. "Unfortunately the very qualities employers look for are the qualities they find lacking in many new graduates. Employers say new graduates lack face to face communication skills. They say many students tend to lack presentation skills, teamwork skills, and overall inter-personal (gets along well with others) skills."

Amen.

The Health Costs: Stressed to Death

As recently as a hundred years ago four out of five of us lived in small towns or the countryside. Today, those numbers are more than reversed. When we're asked to describe country life, we use words like slow, calm, quiet and, admittedly, often dull. Cities, on the other hand, we know to be fast-paced, vibrant, noisy and exciting. What we agree on is that between the city and the country there is an enormous difference in the level of that dis-ease of our age: "stress."

Stress has not only been accepted but embraced as part of the multi-tasking, thrilling new culture. I can imagine future discussions about peoples of past ages: The Romantics, The Victorians, the Moderns, then The Stressed.

Leisure time—time to reflect, create, think fresh thoughts, spend in the company of family and friends—which has been promised to us invention after invention, century after century, is shrinking before our eyes. Study after study finds us slowly blurring the distinction between work and leisure and working longer hours, not to get ahead but just to stay afloat.

So what? you ask. We simply shift gears, speed up, and blast ahead, no problem. Not so.

Researchers in San Francisco recently found that "chronic emotional stress erodes telomerase, an enzyme in our cells that helps extend our life-span, keeping us young and healthy. The cells of the most stressed out women were effectively aged ten years more than normal."

While stress may vary from city to city, it is worth looking at North America's greatest contribution to stress: New York.

In an article entitled "The Ecology of Stress," in *The New York Times*, the writer described New York as "a psychological experiment designed to test the bounds of sanity. Take a few million type-A strivers, jam them into tiny apartments and 50-hour-a-week jobs, deprive them of trees, grass and nature, then have them drink too much and travel around in crammed underground tubes: That is a near perfect environment for over-whelming the allostatic system—the scientific term for bodily processes that help us manage stressful events."

The result is shocking: "In New York, the rate at which people die of heart attacks is 55 percent higher than the national average."

That sounds bad enough in itself when you consider that NYC has some of the best hospitals in the world, and, even more so, when you factor in that the national

average is comprised mainly of other cities. One can easily imagine the enormity of difference between New
York and Penobscot Harbor, Maine.

How suddenly a stressful environment affects us, was
shown in findings by Nicholas Christenfeld, a psychology professor at the University of California. He found
that even for visitors to New York, the heart attack rate
was 34 percent higher than normal. And the reverse
was true: when New Yorkers travel to another part of
the country, their rate drops below the city's norm by 20
percent.

The writer observes, "Turns out your mother was
right: The city really *will* kill you."

Environmental Costs

We seem to have become a society that dreads to look
reality in the face. Perhaps, in our frantic lives, we have
no time for profound consideration; we value rapid recognition, a quick pigeon-holing, then, Wham, we move
on. So those who worry about the kind of world they'll
be leaving to their children are conveniently categorized
and dismissed as "tree-huggers"; those who care about
the health and welfare of their neighbors as "socialists."

Thus environmentalists have become the new *other*.
They are best dismissed, for they keep impeding progress
by reminding us who we really are; and disturbing us with

notions of how great we could be. They remind us that the moment we lost respect for the world around us and invented the idiotic term "man against nature" as if we ourselves were not natural but artificial products, we were emotionally and spiritually doomed. Nature was downgraded to "natural resource" to profit from, at any cost.

And with our minds and hearts closed to past and future, we work and consume without giving real thought to "Why?" The slogan of our age seems to be "Why not?" We don't stop and think, Why do I need a bigger house? A third car? A fourth TV? We buy it because we can squeeze in the payments, because there are a few unused dollars on our last credit card.

We pretend that the things we buy have no past and no future: they are just some objects to be bought, enjoyed, then thrown away. Well they're not. Almost every item we purchase has a long past and often an even longer reckoning; most threaten the environment.

The biggest one that's looming, though deceptively ethereal, is global warming. Whether we like it or not, the majority of the scientific community agrees that CO_2 emissions, mostly from burning fossil fuels, is building up a gas "comforter" over our planet. Since the industrial revolution, when we began gushing CO_2 in earnest, the levels of CO_2 in the atmosphere have gone from 280 parts per million to 390 ppm today. That's a 40% rise, and what's worse is that half of that rise has occurred since the late 1970's. In the words of Columbia University economist Jeffrey D.Sachs, "This is running away." And China and India are—as consumers hence $CO2_2$ gushers—barely getting rolling: per capita China emits one-quarter that of the US, Canada or Dubai.

Scientific opinion does vary on the potential temperature increase before we might manage to bring emissions under control, but 5 or 6 degrees Fahrenheit are considered "mildly optimistic" and a rise as high as 18 degrees cannot be ruled out. That would drastically transform the planet. This is already occurring in the forest behind our house. The majestic century-old oaks are dying, while all around them, heat-loving species of ilex and *corbezzolo* are thriving like never before.

And yet our consumption driven society, still the model for the world, is gushing CO_2 like there is no tomorrow.

To understand how a single, seemingly innocent, and relatively small object is in fact a mega global polluter, let's look at one of the world's favorite pastimes: the video game. Since its inception, about 1.5 *billion* game consoles have been sold, weighing, with packaging, close to 10 billion pounds. Used as roofing tile they could cover Manhattan. Just imagine how much mining, excavating, smelting and manufacturing, drilling and refining, packing and transporting it took to produce that Mount Everest of toys. Imagine the energy consumed at every step, the pollution, the oil spills, the CO_2 emissions just to produce that toy.

Then we, well-meaning parents, without a blink of forethought, drove some great hulking monster to the mall built to display the toy in tasteful, soothing, musical surroundings, with waterfalls and escalators, heating and air-conditioning and lots of pretty lights, all burning up energy and indirectly contributing to the oil spewing into the Gulf of Mexico. And that's a newsworthy spill. Much less known is the Niger Delta where it has been estimated that over the last five decades, the amount of oil spilled equals about 50 times the disaster caused by the Exxon Valdez to the point where local fisherman can no longer sustain families.

And we have only just begun, for the console will require many DVD games. According to Breed Media, the production and transportation of a standard DVD disc produces about 30 pounds of CO_2 per disk and requires much power to run it. The National Resources Defense Council found that game consoles in the US consume 16 billion kilowatt hours per year; enough to power the city of San Diego, malls, stadiums, game consoles and all. To think, for millions of years we lived without it, our kids were happy and healthy playing hide and seek, thrilled by playing tag, or on rainy days sharing a deck of cards or a chessboard.

And video games are just one very small item out of the thousands of goods and gadgets we consume, because for most of the past decade we have done little else but shop. We bought cars, RVs then SUVs, radios, then stereos, then cassettes, then VCRs, then CDs. We bought Instamatics, Veg-a-matics, popcorn-makers, muffin bakers, machines to mow the lawn, fry a prawn, shear the dog, saw a log, to blow snow, leaves, hair or air; we bought gear to spin and barbecue a chicken, broil it, roast it, deep-fry it or toast it, or put it in the microwave and blow it to the moon; we bought chemicals to calm our fits, dry our pits, expand our tits. . . Have we gone and lost our collective bloody minds?

Or are we simply bored? Have our lives become so meaningless and empty that we have to fill each moment with a toy? If that's so, it's sad. Sad that we might turn the universe's most miraculous planet—so wondrous that some of us feel only a god could have made it—into a monstrous monument to boredom.

The good news is that to reverse the trend is child's play. We simply need to replace objects with people. They make us much happier anyway. Numerous studies have found that our greatest daily joy comes from socializing: the intimacy of our lovers, or encounters with family and friends.

It's easy to learn to live well again—we did it when we were children—lived simply, freely and passionately. We just have to revive the exuberant, physically-vigorous, people-loving and fun-loving child in us all.

CHAPTER 7

The Steady Job: Now You See It, Now You Don't

"Job creation has now slowed to a crawl. At the
current pace, it could take 10 years just to replace
the jobs lost during the recession, leading credence
to the idea that the boom years were all a historic
aberration; the new normal is bleak."

—TIMOTHY EGAN, *The New York Times*

The Myth of the Steady Job

I don't think it's an over-statement to say that much
of our lives are spent training, preparing, searching
for, finding and holding onto a steady job. Society and
mom and dad expected us to have it, for then we could
lead a safe and steady life, in the lap of, if not luxury,
then at least comfort. And it was true for a few post-

war decades that once landed, the steady job could be held on to for life as long as we pulled our weight, made an effort, put our best foot forward. While it was also true that we had to say good-bye to our dreams of independence, adventure and whatever spontaneous nomadism we had entertained until then; in exchange we were guaranteed un-varied continuity, an uninter-rupted flow of the weekly paycheck and a respected place in society—not to mention unlimited access to credit cards and the Mall. And after a life of dedicated service, we could take our gold watch and small but steady pension, and move—though we weren't sure why—to the 'burbs of Florida.

To put it another way: we could, after just a short time on the job, sit down and write our autobiography in advance, assured that, except for some minor tweaks, we would pretty well have gotten our whole future right.

Believe me, there is no cynicism intended; I myself once dreamt of a steady job and the accompanying steady life, but found out at a painfully early age—the summer between high-school and university—that I would be, for all my life, absolutely and completely unemployable.

The summer of my "awakening," began with great promise, fulfilling every seventeen-year old guy's dream: cars. Big cars. Lots of cars. Shiny cars. Now, to a passion-less onlooker, washing, cleaning and cut-polishing cars in a less-than-elegant used-car lot might not seem like a covetable career but not only did I get to sit behind the wheel, but, once in a while, I could actually drive.

I loved that job. Fresh air, clean hands, no noise except the music of the car radio, and the growl of the big V-8's when I turned the key. Paradise. I was comfortable, having fun and getting paid for it. Imagine my surprise, when the manager came up to me one morning and told me I was fired. Why? I was dedicated, hard-working, thorough, wasted no wax or rags. I mean what was so wrong with testing brakes and cornering abilities? Were these vital statistics of interest to no one?

Next, I got a job cutting grass. Industrial grass, acres of it, with an aging push-type lawnmower. I didn't mind; I would spend the summer strolling back and forth daydreaming without interruption. The reason for my dismissal the third day was that I had the "wrong attitude" toward low tree branches. I broke one.

Having burned through two careers in the span of three short weeks, the average person would have been disheartened, discouraged or even suicidal standing on the brink of a job-less, credit-less life. But not I. I knew better. I did not interpret these dismissals as failures; instead I saw them as God's way of nudging me to work for someone who would never ever fire me. Me.

Just to make sure, I tried other jobs in the summers that followed. Desk jobs. Silence, air at precisely sixty-eight degrees and my own desk. The first job was for a railroad company, the second for a sailboat builder. The hours were good, the work varied and sociable. Yet, something was wrong. First there was the barely perceptible but exhausting office friction: petty jealousies over desks, windows, typewriters, expenses, bad-mouthing, back-stabbing, the boss looking over my shoulder. But worse was the realization that at the end of each day, I had little to look back on with contentment or pride; the only fulfillment was the Friday paycheck.

And worse was the thought that I might have already lived each day of my life; that I would arrive at that desk at the same time every morning, with an occasional new cushion for the chair and a new typewriter ribbon when I truly earned it.

I was in my early twenties, not only terrified by the thought of my life flowing by uneventfully, but outside my window there were islands and wide oceans, and mysterious countries and far away places—the whole world waiting just for me to see.

I quit. Then, with an amazing lady, built an ocean-going sailboat to sail the seven seas.

PLEASE DON'T THINK me maladjusted or lazy; I have loved working with my hands all my life. At eighteen, I built myself a houseboat using a hand-saw, a hammer, lots of cast-off material, and help from two dear friends. Later, I toiled for a year building that sailboat with Candace. So, for myself or even to help my neighbors, I'll happily work like a draft mule from dawn 'til dusk. I'll haul rocks all day, pile bricks, chop wood, shovel pig shit by the cartload, or load ninety-pound bales of hay on top of a ten-foot stack in hundred-degree weather all morning and again after lunch—better after lunch when I'm full of *prosciutto* pasta, roast pheasant, and wine. I might be a draft mule, but I'm an independent draft mule.

Working on your own means you can live as you please: you get up when you want, and quit work when you want, laugh or bray or sing your heart out all day, or dance around like a damned fool or lie down under a tree. It's up to you. You're free. And you can limit your work to things that permit you to look back at each day with fulfillment and even pride.

MOST OF YOU might dismiss this as the ranting of some idealist who simply doesn't fit into the modern working world. That's probably true. But then where exactly do you yourself fit it? Where and when do you feel wildly happy? Or fiercely alive, or at peace, or even just content? I don't think these emotions are a luxury. They should be the norm among a species that trumpets itself superior to all others both in intellect and spirit. I would think them the norm in anybody's life, and, if they're not, then perhaps he doesn't fit into this world any more than I. If, as it seems, so many of us live the life of a restless drone, if so many of us qualify as Freud's 'civilization's discontents', then perhaps it is not *we* who do not fit into this world, but it is this world that does not fit in with us.

And if this is true, then perhaps it's time we stop changing ourselves to death. Stop changing cars, houses, wives and husbands, the color of our hair, the size of our pecs or our bank accounts. None of these have worked solo or combined. And if all this self-changing has brought no lasting joy, then why do we believe that the next one will? Maybe it's time to leave ourselves alone. Maybe it's time instead to change the world.

Security Not Long Ago

When we lived in the country, our lives had predictable seasons and rhythms interrupted only by occasional hail or drought that destroyed crops and menaced us with shortages until the next year.

The townspeople's lives were even more solid. Craftsmen, shopkeepers, doctors, butchers and bakers all had their firm place in the community, though admittedly none of them got rich, and certainly none got famous.

The city promised to improve on all that. It lured us in with businesses where fortunes could be made; work that required no physical exertion; income not dependent on either sun or rain; careers with fewer working hours; and, above all, a job that was steady.

Indeed steady jobs would be fine if furnishing them, and keeping them exciting, creative, fun and, most importantly, *steady*, were our society's top priority. But it's not.

While the word "jobs" has become a mantra—presidents, congress and the senate live and die by it—and the creation of jobs has justified everything from wars to the destruction of the environment, no way has been found to either reliably create or maintain them.

And yet the worst crime of the myth of the steady job is not that it misleads—it is only steady until you're laid off—but that its endless pursuit preempts the option to lead an independent, varied, and truly secure life. Yet it has become the lifeblood of our system. We even steer our children toward it from an early age. Seemingly innocuous questions like, "What will you be when you grow up?" imprint on vulnerable, impressionable minds that in our culture merely being human is a waste of time, but being a "credit-default swapper" really means a lot.

SO, INSTEAD OF recognizing our genetic need for security, love and friendship, and working full time at satisfying them *directly*, we pour all our energies, both physical and mental, into training for, finding, and clutching a Steady Job. This is not only putting the cart before the horse, it is more like putting it right on top of him. Wouldn't it make infinitely more sense to pour our hearts and soul into building ourselves a home, growing our own food—getting by, finding a lover, and cultivating real friends, while working full-bore at becoming the wisest, kindest, wittiest, most creative human beings we can be? *Then*, if the urge moves us, *only then*, we could go out and get a Steady Job.

The Promise

The four things steady jobs traditionally offered were: lifetime security, continuous advancement with ever-rising wages, fewer working hours, less stress, and at the end of it all, those lazy years in Fort Lauderdale. Oh boy. If you still believe all that, then I have a slightly used bridge in Brooklyn to sell you.

Security

Never have jobs been less secure than today.

We steadfastly focus on the Great Recession that started back in 2007, as if it were a rogue and unique event that tarnished the Golden Century which ended with Lehman's fall. Not so. I don't think it too simple-minded to outline the past one-hundred years like this: Great War I, short party, crash, depression, Great War II, party, recession, recession, market-bubble, recession, tech-bubble, recession, housing-bubble, bust.

Of course jobs were plentiful during World War I,

manpower was low and military production in demand. The crash of '29 and the Depression ended that boom. We clawed out of the Depression on the back of World War II when industry bloomed again to furnish the raging war.

For thirty years after VE day, we partied. Family income, after inflation, doubled, as did the number of cars sold every year. Court cases and divorces doubled too, but when you're having fun, who frets over details. So we bought whatever we could grab, *quintupling* the amount we spent on cosmetics, recreation, and toys. Economic prosperity seemed as if it would never end.

Then it did.

Starting in the Seventies, the road to paradise took a short-cut to hell. Between the recessions of 1972 and 1992 (with the recession of the early '80s in between) wages adjusted for inflation *fell* 20 percent.

The only lasting boom we have had since has been in pollution, and the numbers of the poor and the super rich. Between 1970 and 1989, the number of Americans with incomes of a million dollars or more a year increased from 643 to 61,987—nearly a *hundredfold*. And we had a veritable windfall in the rise of vicious crimes; since the mid-sixties murders doubled, robberies quintupled, aggravated assaults, rapes, and the salaries of corporate CEO's quadrupled.

The "downsizings" of the early '90s taught steady jobs believers lessons in cruel reality. Xerox announced a

20 percent trim of its white collar positions; Sears Roe-buck cut 33,000 employees; IBM 20,000 in addition to the 65,000 it had eliminated in three years; banks and S&Ls slashed 50,000 jobs; and General Motors, instead of the normal annual bonus, announced on December 18, 1991 the permanent termination of 70,000 long-standing positions. Merry Christmas! One laid-off vice-president, whose banker wife also got the falling ax, summed up the stunned reaction of the country in *The New York Times*, "Can you believe it? We both got into this thinking we were set for life."

The recession of 2001 was followed by a "jobless recovery" in which millions of jobs were outsourced to India and China.

Many of those who still had jobs paid a heavy price. In the period from 2001 to 2003, about 5.3 million work-ers were displaced from 'long-tenure' jobs (those held 3 years or longer), and two thirds of those who then found new jobs had taken pay and benefit cuts in the process.

The Great Recession hit like a ton of bricks. Over 8 million jobs were lost, and two years later we're still get-ting nowhere. There are, at writing, 15 million unem-ployed in the US. If we add in their dependents, old and young, we come up with more than 30 million people. That's as if not a single person—man, woman or child—in Ireland, Denmark, Norway, Finland, Switzerland and Austria had any visible means of support.

What is even sadder is that if jobs were created at the pace of 100,000 a month—the largest monthly leap since the recession began—to recover the eight million lost would take us close to 2020.

Rising Wages and Advancement

Contradicting the myth that wages will climb yearly and advancement is just ahead, around the corner, is the following comment by Lawrence Katz, a Harvard economist. He summed up the first ten years of the twenty-first century with, "We have basically lost a decade. We had a plutocratic boom then we had an equalitarian recession. Taken together only the top ends up growing... For the typical American family, the 2000s have been a disaster."

Not only was it the first decade since the 1930s with zero net job creation, (every other had job growth of at least 20 percent) but to put "the disaster" in plain numbers, the median household income—the amount earned by a family at the exact center of the income scale, sank from $51,300 in 1998 to $50,300 in 2008. What's more depressing is that this decrease occurred while the economy expanded and worker productivity went up. This financial stall was the first time since World War II that the typical family was worse off at the end of an economic *expansion* than at the start.

As Katz observed, the benefits of the expansion landed in the pockets of a very few. The top 1 percent of families, those with over $382,000 yearly income (who also control 70 percent of total US assets) stashed away "about 75 percent of the total growth." Some growth did trickle down, but mostly to the next 9 percent of families who pocketed "almost half of all income" in 2006, the highest share since 1917.

And lest you were worried about those who truly control our lives—no not the insipid politicians but the jackals of finance—in 2007 the average raise of the top thirty CEO's was 1,000 percent. Yes, Virginia, you read right.

That was of course chump-change to Mr. Richard Fairbank CEO of the bank Capital One who chuckled off with a raise of 46,000 percent. And a Mr. Fuld, who did such an immaculate job of driving Lehman Brothers out of existence, pocketed a nifty $71 million.

Finally Mr. Angelo Mozilo, whose Country Wide Financial was one of the true hyenas of the sub-prime loans fiasco, reported enormous losses then took home a measly $124 million. Now if America was truly a charitable country, it would be passing around poor Mr. Mozilo's hat. If it were a wise country, Mr. Mozilo's head would still be in it.

This is in addition to the fact that, as I said, since the seventies real average wages adjusted for inflation have actually fallen. The most pronounced fall occurred during the last two years, and, strangely enough, to those "in their prime earning years between the ages of 45 and 54. Their median income was down 7 percent."

So if you are looking for a steady increase in wages due to your intelligence or diligence or both, I'm afraid the steady job is not the place to start.

Fewer Working Hours and Less Stress

The dream of working less and enjoying it more was dashed along with those of security and rising wages. "Instead of technology being a time-saver," says Warren Bennis, professor at University of Southern California and author of such management classics as *On Becoming a Leader*, "Everybody I know is working harder and longer."

This is borne out by the numbers, especially among college educated men—who, one would suppose, make most use of technology in the workplace: one third of them regularly log 50 hour work-weeks. That is a 50 percent jump since 1980.

When you couple this with our ever-lengthening commutes—LA, Denver and Boston all average an hour, and OMG, even Honolulu clocks in at 54 minutes—then you can see how dangerously close we are getting to what can be considered 11 hour workdays.

AS FOR STRESS, it arises not just from the longer and more frantic working hours, but also from the constant fear of being laid off. This additional stress of course spikes during recessions.

In a CBS News/*New York Times* Poll conducted in February, 2010, almost 60 percent of Americans said they were concerned that someone in their household might lose a job in the next year, including 31 percent who were "very" concerned about this prospect.

THE STRESS OF losing a job has been found to take a significant toll on health. At the extreme, "it doubles the risk of suicide, depression, and attempted suicide."

Michael Luo quoted a Yale study in *The New York Times* in 2010 that showed layoffs more than doubling the risk of heart attack and stroke among older workers. Another study by Kate W. Strully, found that "a person who lost a job, had an 83 percent greater chance of developing a stress-related health problem, like diabetes, arthritis or psychiatric issues."

Luo goes on. "In the most sobering finding, a study published last year found that layoffs can affect life expectancy. The researchers examined death records and earnings data in Pennsylvania during the recession of the early 1980s and concluded that death rates among high-seniority male workers jumped by 50 percent to 100 percent in the year after a job loss, depending on the worker's age. Even 20 years later, deaths were 10 percent to 15 percent higher. That meant a worker who lost his job at age 40 had his life-expectancy cut by a year to a year and a half."

Derek Bok points out a frequently cited study in which job-loss, as a downer, outranked both divorce and separation. The same study found that even when workers find a new position at similar pay, they often fail to regain their earlier form of happiness.

EVEN MORE UNNERVING is a recent finding by Sarah A. Burgard, a professor of sociology and epidemiology at the University of Michigan, who noted that " 'persistent perceived job insecurity' was itself a powerful predictor of poor health and might even be more damaging than actual job loss."

The anxiety among 260 remaining workers at a steel plant in Buffalo was so high after one part of it closed, that two of the remaining workers committed suicide.

AN UNEXPECTED STATISTIC attesting to the damage economic uncertainty can cause, is the recession's effect on our children. Not only do our children become depressed, aggressive or moody, but during this recession there has also been an increase in the rate of child abuse across the country.

Alice Park in *Time* Magazine, quoted analyzed data on 512 cases of head trauma in children's centers of four hospitals, in Pittsburg, Cincinnati, Columbus and Seattle, and found that the number of cases had increased 50 percent since December 2007.

She goes on to describe the head injuries resulting from shaken baby syndrome as those that "occur to young children when frustrated parents shake their children in an effort to quiet their crying or stop tantrums. The force of the motion causes the child's brain to shift violently in the skull, crushing blood vessels and damaging still developing tissue. It is a desperate act, one that tends to surface as a knee-jerk response by a stressed parent."

OUR DREAMS OF a bright future are turning into nightmares of insecurity and stress. We seem to be caught on a runaway train of a system which anthropologist Colin Turnbull described as one of "cutthroat economics, where almost any kind of exploitation and degradation of others, impoverishment and ruin, is justified in terms of an expanding economy and the consequent confinement of the world's riches in the pockets of a few."

Why the system goes on without people yelling "Enough!" is perhaps our greatest mystery. Maybe my friend, Mr. Bradley from Pender Island, was right when he said, "We are all asleep while the world slips from under us."

You might say I'm focused on the negative, that things will get better, that there is light at the end of the tunnel. I would humbly ask you, "What light?" According to an essay by Nobel Prize economist Paul Krugman, we are in the tunnel to stay. He writes, "We are now, I fear, in the early stages of a third depression. It will probably look more like the Long Depression than the much more severe Great Depression. But the cost—to the world economy and, above all, to the millions of lives blighted by the absence of jobs—will nonetheless be immense."

That a change is needed is beyond doubt. How profound it has to be is hard to say, but as B. Drummond Ayres in a *New York Times* essay concluded with such foresight two decades ago, "What remains is a nagging doubt about the strength and viability of American capitalism and, for that matter, the viability of the whole American system of government."

I venture to expand that to the global system of government.

Perhaps it is time, as Maureen Dowd suggested, to man the barricades. Or if not, it's certainly high-time we began looking after ourselves.

CHAPTER 8

Gone Fishin'

I TRUST YOU have divined by now that in these times of crippling unemployment, hectic family life, and insecure future, one logical improvement may be a shorter work-week. I don't mean going to work less so we can watch the *The Poker Channel*, or try to get our Facebook friend numbers up into five digits, I mean having more time to work on providing ourselves with true security, to spend with our children, and lead a physically active, invigorating life.

True Security

I think we can, without sounding dimwittedly simplistic, narrow the reasons we go to work every morning down to two major ones: to put a roof over our heads and food on the table. We also need cash to buy rags to cover our privates and tip our manicurist, but let's just stick to the basics.

Would we not feel less vulnerable if we could guarantee ourselves abundant and healthy food no matter what the GDP in China, or which banks or hedge funds are breathing their last today? Would we not feel stronger growing and raising a good part of our own food? And would we not feel much more secure, if instead of shouldering some monstrous mortgage all our lives, staying one step ahead of foreclosure, we could build a small house with our own two hands and help from friends and family, and soon own it out-right?

With some extra days a week we could do both.

First, a garden, which any yard could provide, could grow enough fruit, vegetables and even fish in a pond to turn you into a green-grocer and fishwife. As to how good that feels, let me quote Candace who said, unprompted, just the other day: "I remember the first time I had a full vegetable garden and our fruit trees were in bloom. I looked at them and the thought came to me, 'My God, this is real wealth.' "

Apart from security, I don't think we need dwell on how much more healthy physical activity like digging, hoeing and gathering is than stuffing a box into the microwave. One day a week of work would easily keep a food garden going (more on this in a later chapter and the appendix) and not just for maintenance but for all those other cool family activities like making jams, preserves, and a Mount Everest of pies and cookies.

. . .

AS FOR BUILDING your own house, I know the very thought of it strikes terror into your heart. It shouldn't. Current North American frame construction of two-by-fours, press-board, sheetrock and fake siding, could be learned in one year of high-school; or, if you're past school age, I can teach you all the tasks in about a day. Take it from someone who, with no skills, has cobbled together two houseboats, a world-cruising sailboat, a four story cedar-and-glass ocean-front house, and restored a thirteenth century friary in Tuscany. If I could do it, believe me, so can you.

Learning how to use a tape-measure, square and pencil takes about ten minutes; how to cut straight with a circular saw: one hour; how to bang nails without bending them or crushing your left thumb: two hours; how to cut sheet-rock with a utility knife: ten minutes; how to apply a tourniquet to the gash in your leg: twenty minutes. Any questions? Good, then let's go grab some lunch. We'll talk more about building our home later.

Full Employment

When the 2007 Great Recession hit, pink slips rained down on eight million Americans. In Germany the sky stayed blue. Instead of terminating long-held positions, firms did something more humane; they shared the pain.

To adjust to the lower demand, many cut back working hours, with the result that no one suffered the worry and humiliation of a lay-off; the companies survived the market slump; and no skilled and experienced employee was lost so that when the rebound does come—at writing in spring of 2011 the German GDP gained 3.6 percent, the strongest increase in pan-German history—production can pick up pace without a hitch.

As David Leonhardt wrote recently, "The jobs slump has become too severe to disappear anytime soon. But there is no reason to treat it as a problem that's immune from solutions. For starters, it would be worth figuring out what other countries are doing right."

If time-sharing worked for two years in Germany, why not try it here?

More time with kids during week

The Dutch, ever a sensible and practical people (as in "going Dutch") have been experimenting for years with shorter work-weeks. With the economic crisis they are "turning part-time culture from a weakness into a strength."

The New York Times cited some interesting new statistics. "Seventy-five percent of Dutch women now work part time, compared to 41 percent in other European Union countries and 23 percent in the United States. Twenty-three percent of Dutch men have reduced hours, compared to 10 percent across the European Union and in the United States; another nine percent work a full week in four days."

Note: the average American works about 350 more hours a year—that's nine weeks' worth—than most Europeans.

The result is that with parents' days off staggered, many Dutch children spend only three days in day care instead of five with the obvious advantage that the majority of a child's life is based in the family not in public care.

Some Dutch are very strongly anti-day care so they bring in the grandparents to fill what gaps remain.

Just imagine how much more secure a child would feel having spent most of his or her initial years in the nurturing and comforting ambience of home instead of in generally impersonal public institutions.

And time with them could be more constructive; we could help with their school-work, spend more "quality-time," and get a head start on teaching them to be independent: how to run the food garden, and even help us in the building of our house.

All that would provide them not only with self-confidence and pride, but with a real childhood and home-made memories, not the virtual, store bought kind of watching Lady Gaga or twitching their joystick playing *Crush the Pedestrians*.

A Real Weekend

With more days of flexible time for doing all the chores we spend our weekends doing now, we could indulge in true weekend weekends of fishing and hiking trips, outings or gatherings of the memorable kind. Not only would we become infinitely more tightly knit as couples, lovers or families, but the varied experiences would make us more interesting people, with broader knowledge, wider points of view, and much greater appreciation for nature and each other.

Couples with children could perhaps rekindle their barely smoldering romance, by having more time to get away, and relive those special moments alone, when only the other mattered.

Save cost

The savings would be notable, both for the individual and the corporations. Sharing the work week would allow us to share work-space much as Bloomberg News does now in their ultra-modern building with unassigned desks which in truth are use-as-you-need work stations. Cutting the daily commute would be a vast improvement to the commuters, our over-strained infrastructure, the cities that need to provide them; and to our poor environment which at the moment is on its knees from the tsunami of cars.

I'm sure a hundred objections could be raised; dozens of logistical problems to be solved, but isn't that what dreams are for? Don't dreams lead to our most noble inventions as they allow us, indeed force us, to imagine a new way, to invent something wonderful, to create or recreate and in the end come up with a more humane, hopeful and gratifying life, not just for us today, but one we can bequeath with pride to our children.

CHAPTER 9

TGIM—Thank Goodness It's Monday!

WHILE WE'RE INCREASING the time and quality of home life, why not revamp the places where we work?

It seems to me that the principal aim of any business enterprise is—or, at least in my naïve mind, should be—first, to produce something of the best possible quality that in some way truly betters the human condition, and, second, to provide a decent and dignified living for all involved.

Now that you've finished laughing and rolling on the floor, you can get up and listen for a minute.

As far as I can tell, much of world business is run in a completely bizarre manner, which to someone looking in from the outside seems not only perverse, and in the long term counterproductive, but also offensive to humanity. First, the questions of quality and the bettering the human condition seem alien to any business model. The priority goes to profit margin, marketability, and growth. In plain words, the main concern is: what's the maximum that can be pocketed by pushing a product to as great a number of people as possible while paying those who actually produce it as little as possible.

This mentality is due to a flaw that by now dominates our culture: the non-participating, absentee owner. Here's an example.

There is a scene in an old John Ford movie of Oklahoma sharecroppers being evicted from the land their families had worked for seventy years. One begs the evicting sheriff to understand his love of the place and to let him stay, so he can eke out a living and feed his family. The sheriff says he'd like to help but can't because his orders come from the administrator in Omaha, and the administrator can't help because his orders came from the owner in San Francisco, who can't help either because his orders come from the banker in New York, who can't help because he's too busy helping himself. I might have blown some details but I'm sure you get the gist.

Our entire system of ownership, not just of land but also of businesses and corporations, has become about as ethereal as this movie scene. Most owners are nowhere near where the actual production is being done; hence an owner-worker relationship—one that would enable all to truly work together for everyone's maximum good—rarely exists.

So, mostly unwittingly, absentee owners not only create and support some dismal working conditions but also dump millions of gallons of herbicides and pesticides on their lands, while at their distant suburban homes they wear "Save the Planet" buttons and separate their trash. Others, who have killed thousands with coal dust or asbestos, or, with oil-wells, poison the Gulf of Mexico, sit on their yachts and celebrate the environmental beneficence of sailing.

On the human front, absentee owners, without the blink of an eye, throw tens of thousands of employees onto the street to insure their own profits, but on Sunday morning slip a dollar onto the collection plate to help the suffering poor.

The truth is, with modern diversified portfolios, investment bank mutual funds, and hundreds of mostly indecipherable financial instruments, the absentee owners of today are, as Mick Jagger sang in *Sympathy for the Devil*, "you and me."

AS THINGS STAND, most of us "owners"—distant shareholders, whether through our own investment, or insurance fund, or pension fund—haven't a clear idea of what exactly we own. Since a CEO's primary concern is to keep his job by maximizing the profits of the anonymous owners, it is small wonder that the workers, who produce, get little attention if any. Ultimately, they are listed under the "expense" column, whose reduction is the main aim of any good CEO.

Now, no matter how hard I try, I cannot believe that this state of affairs was ever anyone's dream. And if it wasn't our dream, then why has it been allowed to so thoroughly bugger up our lives?

I don't think we need a long list of examples or details. It seems only too obvious that if those who *made* the real decisions had to physically *live* with them and thus suffer the consequences, disasters like Bhopal, Love Canal or the oil spill in the Gulf of Mexico, would never happen, and we would be living in a much safer world. And if the owners actually lived and worked among workers, their welfare and the welfare of their families would be of much greater concern. Who wouldn't agree that, if a personal bond existed between employer and employee, the concern for each would be greater, and the loyalty, the commiseration, and the working toward common goals and common gain would be substantially enhanced?

TO CREATE A healthier, more socially secure world, two simple practices should be encouraged. Neither is new; both have been globally successful for centuries.

One is the employee-owned company; the other, the live-on-premises-family business.

The Employee-Owned Company

W.W. Norton & Company on Fifth Avenue, across from the stately New York Public Library, is one of America's most respected book publishers. The firm was founded by Mr. and Mrs. Norton in 1923. After her husband's death in 1945, Mrs. Norton, choosing not to sell the company to outsiders, agreed to sell her stock to the senior employees regardless of how long it might take for them to pay. To assure stability and security, an agreement was drawn up among the shareholders restricting stock ownership to *active* employees. Those retiring or leaving for any other reason have to sell their shares back to the company. So, when Norton has a stockholders' meeting, most employees attend.

The results have been remarkable. Not only are job security and employees' attitudes infinitely better than at other publishers—according to people who have moved to Norton from other esteemed houses—but the quality of the books produced is consistently high. Norton is a medium-sized company, but it has become renowned for the subject matter and the authoritativeness of its books, as exemplified by *The Norton Anthology of English Literature* in the college department, and authors like Nobel Prize winner Paul Krugman and Michael Lewis in trade. Both in academia and trade publishing, Norton is generally considered to be among the three best. There are, of course, publishing houses with traditional forms of ownership that have remained successful over decades, but not in such a congenial atmosphere. I am not exaggerating when I say that the staff feel and behave like a family. This reassuring ambiance, not only allows people to thrive, but it also attracts the best people from other houses. As a senior designer who moved to Norton from a most respected art-book publisher observed, "I have never worked with such an intelligent group of people."

Because there is so little pressure, backstabbing, politicking, jockeying for power or for extra paper clips—the officers get no company cars, assistants are shared, the offices are tiny, and the furnishings are unpretentious hand-me-downs—more time and energy can be spent in creative and productive ways. And because almost everyone has a share in the company, the pride that goes into the work is the kind one usually finds with craftsmen working for themselves. So, people stay. The head of production retired last year after forty years, a number of editors have put in over thirty, the head of marketing, and the current president the same. Since 1923, there have been only five presidents and four treasurers. The general book sales staff has been there for an average of fifteen years. At Norton, if you have been on the staff less than ten, you are considered a rookie.

NORTON IS THE kind of place where if you need help, you only have to ask. When the head of a division was about to be married to someone whose work was based in Chicago, she went to the president to tell him regretfully that she had to leave. His response was, "*You* are the division. Take it with you." She did. When an editorial assistant was having family problems necessitating lengthy time off, Norton told her she could come back when she was ready. And when Norton people feel stifled in their jobs, the company tries to find them something more challenging to do. Events like these create an atmosphere of security that is the antithesis of most corporations, where it is normal to go home happy on Friday only to come back on Monday to a cleaned out desk and a check for two weeks' severance pay.

The fact that there is no ownership pressure for mega-profits has allowed Norton to be run by editors instead of by money-men. In the daily workings of the company, this translates into books judged by measures other than maximum profitability. Because of the absence of the threat of dismissal and the pressure to out-perform others, editors often publish their convictions—what they feel to be vital in humanitarian, intellectual or artistic terms. Hence, the Norton list is noticeably short on flashy titles, perhaps to the detriment of short-term balloon profits, but to the enhancement of long-term integrity, which translates into profit of a more lasting kind. None of this is written in policy papers. There are none at Norton; things seem to diffuse by osmosis. And just what constitutes a good Norton book no one can say, but everyone seems to know. Highly respected works by Lewis, Krugman, and Carl Jung, graced the Norton list in 2009, and while the rest of the publishing world was quietly imploding, Norton had its best fiscal year.

How profitable the house is, is kept confidential, but it has continued through more than three quarters of a century, with no upheavals or disasters, no great mergers, reorganizations or vicious cutting of employees, and has provided a good living for everyone involved.

Along with the money, Norton gave those who worked there an indelible, and justifiable, sense of pride, and a sense that, throughout the years, they were respected and cared for; they belonged. In a society driven almost exclusively by the rush for profit, a society where humanity is an expendable cost—to be cared for, to belong, is perhaps the most cherished reimbursement of all.

WHILE THE NORTON ownership was set up decades ago, a relatively new provision ESOP—employee stock ownership plan—helps company employees buy out existing owners.

As to how these employee-owned firms perform compared to the rest of the corporate world is highlighted in a recent study from Georgetown University. The research found that during the recession year of 2008, ESOP firms' revenue grew an average of 15.1 percent, compared to a *decline* of 3.4 percent for all private-industry revenue. ESOP firms also showed employment growth (*plus* 2 percent, as opposed to *minus* 2.8 percent in overall US private employment), faster wage growth (5.9 percent compared with 3 percent) and higher wages during 2008.

Another new provision by congress: the S-ESOP (retirement savings plan) was found to "give S-ESOP workers a more secure retirement by providing substantial retirement savings for employee-owners, in this case at a time when most other companies did not. Surveyed S-ESOP companies increased contributions to retirement benefits for employees by 18.6 percent, while other U.S. companies increased their contributions to employee retirement accounts by only 2.8 percent."

Mark Lewis, president of Woodfold, Inc., in Forest Grove, Oregon, summed up the ESOP success well when he said, "When times are tough, employee-owners work smarter and harder because of their commitment and investment in the business and this makes us stronger."

One great success story has been the accolade winning King Arthur Flour Company, which supplies baking tools and ingredients. Founded in Boston in 1790, it has grown from a family owned mail-order business with only five employees as recently as 1990, to the nearly 800 strong today. The company is a 100 percent employee-owned and known nationwide for its purity and consistent quality.

The Wall Street Journal named it one of the Top 15 Small Workplaces for 2008. The recognition identifies "exceptional employers that foster teamwork, flexibility, high productivity and innovation while also treating their employees with respect, providing opportunities for professional growth and advancement, and providing benefits, both traditional and nontraditional, that make the employee experience better growth."

The Live-on-the-Premises Family Business

I was eleven in 1956 when, after the Russian army crushed the Hungarian revolution, I escaped with my mother and her friend to Austria and spent the first week in a refugee camp. The three of us together had six dollars. One day, a well-dressed gentleman came in and said he needed an experienced textile-dyer. The nineteen year-old street kid we had befriended at the border immediately raised his hand. That he had worked only as a gardener didn't give him pause. The gentleman said he would like to take him to Vienna to meet the factory owner. The street kid asked if he could take me along because I was his brother.

Both he and my mother ended up working at the textile-dyeing factory owned by the Family Edlinger.

The factory was at the end of the street adjoining the Danube marshlands. From the street it looked like the other brick apartment buildings, but inside was the plant. Beside it, facing the river, were apartments for the employees. Across from the gate, facing the street, were the apartments of the Edlinger family. When we arrived, they all came out to greet us.

The place was spotless. Trees and flowers everywhere, the plant was clean, no fumes, no smells, no intrusive noises. The workers who lived in the apartment building were friends. They played soccer on a half-frozen field together, they ice-fished together, worked little vegetable gardens together across the street. I was too young to note social interaction but I do remember people speaking with pride about where they lived and worked, and an atmosphere of general good spirits.

The Edlinger model is similar to most company-run towns in North America, but the big difference was that the owners lived and worked as close to the plant as any employee, breathed the same air, suffered the same noise, and saw working and living conditions with their own eyes every day. And, as important, they saw their workers in the shops, the bars, the streets, and got to know them, not just as impersonal cogs in a well-oiled factory wheel, but as individuals with families, children, problems, needs and joys. They got to know them routinely, and thoroughly as people. To me, that makes all the difference in the world.

CHAPTER 10

Honor Thy Vegetable Garden

OUR RELATIONSHIP WITH food defines cultures, often starts and decides wars, and reflects not only our social status but our whole economy. It is also a profoundly emotional and social one as when we share meals with friends and family, and when we build comforting memories with our children.

Perhaps the oldest and most enduring food culture is that of China. The Chinese philosopher Lin Yutang wrote, "If there is anything we are serious about it is neither religion nor learning, but food."

To the Chinese, food and friends are inseparable.

Twenty-five-hundred years ago, Confucius dreamed and fussed about the art of cooking and enjoyment of life through the cultivation of the palate and delight of the senses. The art of cooking was much more than food; his culinary etiquette, social sharing, presentation and combining, are still considered to be the standards of today. (As is the cutting of food into bite-size pieces during preparation to avoid the need for knives—for obvious reasons—at the table.) He considered food as one of the beautiful and gentle things which contribute to the peace and harmony of society. His philosophy elevated cooking and eating from a dull daily chore to not only an art form but a celebration of life.

I THINK IT is safe to say that our modern hurry-up culture has, in the past few decades, handily reversed that trend. We seem to grab any industrially made who-knows-what from wherever we can, then eat it, largely alone; on the run or even while we drive; eat it out of paper boxes, and plastic cups, or a dripping package; often while multitasking or watching the tube; seldom giving a thought to the food's appearance or flavor—which, considering what we mostly eat, is not such a bad idea.

For some ancient peoples from the Greeks to the Etruscans, symposia—discussions involving eating, drinking, music and dance—*were* the main thing in life. The culture of food—not just its consumption, but also its growing and preparation—has remained the foundation of life for the Etruscan descendants in today's Tuscany.

While we North Americans were brought up to consider true security to be the steady job, a house, and a cushy pension (all three of which the last recession blew into the "Santa Claus/Easter Bunny" folder), our Tuscan friends have a completely different view of life.

When I asked my neighbor Ofelio, who just celebrated his seventy-sixth birthday, what made him feel secure, he recited a short list: a stack of aged fire-wood for the winter; half a pig put up in the cellar and freezer; a hundred liters of olive oil in a stainless vat; two barrels of wine; chickens and Guinea hens in the courtyard; then he raised his hoe and pointed down the hill at a vast vegetable garden, "And that." And slammed his hoe back into the ground.

Ofelio has a Buddhist mentality to life: when he walks, he walks. And when he hoes, he hoes. His vegetable garden didn't have raised beds or manicured paths; it was absolutely and completely utilitarian. It had big patches of onions, garlic, potatoes, and chard, rows of poled tomatoes, peppers, fennel, carrots, eggplant and zucchini, in fact just about every vegetable I can name.

He grinned at me with pride. "*E il resto del mondo?*" and he leaned his hoe against his chest to free up both his hands, then gave the world an energetic Neapolitan salute.

AND WITH HIM as with most Tuscans, the vegetable garden, the orchard, the olive trees, and the vines are almost always family affairs. Kids, uncles, aunts, nephews all come to help out during the *vendemmia,* or the pig-killing, or to pick olives or share in the bounty of the gardens. It gives children from a very young age a sense of identity, skilled hands, and a sense of belonging.

Since these gardens are such wonders, and the culture of food is such an all-inclusive, gastronomic and social wonder, why don't we all have Ofelio's garden in our yards? What happened to America's once favorite hobby that also gave us fresh, organically pure and nourishing food?

A recent piece in *The Globe and Mail* cited twenty-five foods for health and longevity: almonds, avocados, beets, berries, black beans, broccoli, cabbage, dark chocolate, flaxseed, garlic, green tea, kale, lentils, oats, olive oil (extra virgin), oranges, pomegranates, red bell peppers, red grapes (I substitute red wine and lots of it), salmon, spinach, sweet potatoes, tomatoes, and walnuts.

Now, unless you live on the North Pole, you can grow most of these in any normal yard with the aid of a modest greenhouse. I admit the salmon is a toughie, the olive oil you'll have to buy from us, the green tea from China, and I haven't a clue what the hell flaxseeds are, but the rest are a shoo-in. So why are we all inside lying on the couch instead of outside digging?

The National Gardening Association claims a quarter of American households grow some of their own fruits, vegetables, herbs and berries, so why not the other three quarters? Why is the money spent on lawn-care products ten times more than money spent on the home vegetable garden? When the reasons for having one are so compelling—58 percent of gardeners said they do it for better-tasting food, 54 percent to save money on food bills, 51 percent for better quality food, 48 percent to grow food they know is safe—why is the vegetable garden not a coast to coast fixture?

The Joy of Soil

Twenty years ago a *Los Angeles Times* survey on favorite pastimes found over 60 percent of those questioned put gardening at the top, and while most of the guys probably meant doing wheelies on their lawnmowers, that's still a huge difference from a recent CNN survey, where in a quarter million responses, gardening didn't even make it into the top ten.

Yet many of our friends in big cities from New York to Milan still have a common aspiration: to own a square of dirt, and to get out on a Sunday morning, grab a spade, and dig. The need to have contact with the earth seems hardwired in our genes, if you don't believe me stick your toddler in the yard with a little spade and watch her become instantly a busy, tireless mole. She'll dig feverishly and—almost guaranteed—she'll start "planting" leaves and sticks in the tilled ground.

. . .

THE URGE TO work the land seems to stick with us even in the most inhospitable places, almost no matter how unused to working the land we may be.

The countryside near Siena is hard and dry in late summer. With the wheat cut, the hills are bare and only small vineyards, olive groves and wooded ditches break the brownness of the land. We were taking a Sunday walk on a silent, dusty road, hadn't passed a soul for an hour—there were only ruins in this valley—when amidst some olive saplings, we saw a middle aged man, in shorts and a tennis shirt, hoeing happily around the tree trunks.

He was bright and cheerful, a director of the Bank of Tuscany in Siena, who loves tennis and soccer, but, most of all, he loves digging dirt. He proudly showed us the patch of sorghum he planted for wild pheasants, the woods where he cleared the undergrowth and hoed shallow troughs among the poplars to drain off the water to create an ideal habitat for truffles; but most of all he showed us his grove of olive saplings, planted by his own hands. If you looked really closely, you could see the first cluster of tiny, pale green olives. He talked about growing things—vegetables, figs, anything you can eat. "When you see the first fruit come out on something you have planted, it is such an . . . " he searched for words. "Such an immense joy!"

Thanks to Candace who is the heart and soul (and callouses) behind our three vegetable gardens, we are able to celebrate a harvest nearly every day. To try and compare rationally anything you grew—planted, watered, nursed, protected from evil, watched ripen—with some fruit or vegetable grown elsewhere on this planet is a hopeless task; the others don't have a snowball's chance in hell. Yours, blemished and misshapen as they may be, will be sweeter, richer, have flavors never imagined, while the others will be a watery, tasteless, barely edible pulp.

I look forward each summer's day to just before lunch, when I go out to the garden and pick the darkest, reddest tomatoes I can find. To bite into a homegrown, fully ripe tomato with the warmth of the sun still on it, is—well, what can I say—such an immense joy!

Fresh peas rolling out of the shell, or radishes just uprooted full of all the flavors that they have drawn out of the earth, or the apricot that you watch for days on end waiting for that perfect, ripest moment when it's about to fall, when, as you touch it, it tumbles into your palm, warm, soft, full of nectar. That first bite—good God—is well worth waiting the whole year for.

Bye-Bye Miss American Lawn

There is a sense of vitality to food gardens, plants crowding, fruits bulging, colors exploding, things flowering, maturing, wilting, dying off, the autumn earth freshly tilled, and everything you touch, everything you see, you can eat. And, just as important, someone is out there planting, hoeing, tilling, in touch with the soil and with the cycles of nature.

So why do we pay astronomical sums for, over-processed, over-packaged, often insipid food, transported to us over thousands of miles when much of it we could have grown right in our own yard with much more joy and much less effort, pollution, and expense than it takes to cut, water, and fertilize the useless bloody lawn.

Who will have enough sense and intestinal fortitude to be the first to dig up the lawn and plant in its place a lovely patch of spuds? You can probably do it under one of two conditions: if you're self-confident and just don't give a damn, or if you're armed with enough facts to convince your gasping neighbors.

There seem to be four excellent reasons to lay waste to the lawn: economic, nutritional, environmental and social, so let's touch on them one by one.

Economic Benefit

Last year, CNN cited a report concluding that a family will get an average 25-to-1 return on its investment in a garden. By that count, a family that spends $200 on a medium-to-large garden, as Michelle Obama reportedly did, will save $5,000 in grocery bills over the course of a year.

According to the National Research Council, which is part of the National Academy of Sciences in Washington D.C., the American family spends between 10 and 50 percent of their income on food. This broad range is created by the disparity in annual incomes, such that a family of four with an income of $20,000 spends as much as 50 percent on food, while the family earning $100,000 spends about 10 percent.

These figures bring up an interesting question. In the case of the poorest families, we can assume that the jobs they hold are not of the dream variety. Parking cars and flipping burgers, are probably not on anybody's wish list. If one-half of the earnings from these endeavors goes to pay for food, would it not make more sense to cut the time spent doing them in half, and instead—with much less effort—work a nice food garden?

The objection will be raised that most of the poor have no plot of land in which to plant a garden. I'm glad you brought that up because it's time to change the world to make sure that they do.

The simple argument for that goes like this. To physically survive, our species needs three things: air, water and food. The air has, at least until now, been democratically divided; water, though often impure, is available to most. Is it then not obvious that each of us should be given some access to food? I don't mean given food; just a piece of land in which to grow it. Now the Koch Brothers (who inherited every penny of their billions) would rabidly object that this would be communism. But that would be stupid; in communism no one owns anything; I'm, instead, suggesting that everyone own something.

Until that time comes, we can begin with small steps like a roof-garden. Cities abound with flat roofs, ideal for the shallow six-inch beds needed to grow vegetables. The layer of soil provides two added benefits: insulation against heat and cold, and longevity, offering roofing materials protection from the sun.

Another alternative food source popping up in cities across the globe is the community garden. Our niece in North Vancouver is involved in three major projects promoting community gardening to ensure that residents—especially those in need—have access to a safe, reliable food source. One is an urban garden in the local safe house for youth, where the kids are involved in planting, growing and at the end, getting "free food."

She is also heading the Edible Garden Project, which supports the growing and distribution of local food, and, perhaps most interestingly, she helped to break ground for Vancouver's first urban farm. On a piece of unused parkland donated by the city council, they'll be able to produce and sell organic vegetables right in the city.

. . .

AN ALREADY IN use idea is community-supported agriculture (CSA) While it's not as satisfying as pulling a carrot out of the ground or picking a ripe peach in your own backyard, the system delivers seasonal fresh fruits and vegetables (and, now, even meat, eggs and flowers) that are pesticide-free and competitively priced. This food network—started in Europe and Japan in the '60s—is over 10,000 farms strong in the U.S. alone, and growing. Members share the risk and reward of each harvest by funding a transparent annual budget. This allows farmers to plan ahead and enforces a fair pricing system. Typical small, independent CSA farms sell their vitamin-packed tomatoes or juicy squash at farmers' markets, or provide for pickups or even home deliveries. You may not know to cook kohlrabi or what to do with three pounds of zucchini, but you'll soon find out.

Because the model champions local farms, produce is not shipped or transported across long distances, which helps reduce pollution and costs. CSAs also foster a gratifying producer-consumer relationship: members know who is growing their food and how; which crops thrived this autumn or spring; and from where the turnips have traveled to arrive on their doorstep.

SOME WILL ARGUE that planting a food garden will provide minimal savings because they eat very little fruit or vegetables. This bad habit is understandable if you don't want to live long (remember the twenty-five foods for health and longevity), and is nearly justifiable given the bland produce sold at most supermarkets. How can anyone be enthusiastic over lettuce and tomatoes when they have no more flavor than the average tablecloth?

I confess I used to have very little interest in eating green produce until we moved to Paris and began shopping at a street market twice a week. My enthusiasm did not bloom into a mania until we moved to Italy and Candace began to feed us from the garden. Once I was introduced to *real* fruit and vegetables, I not only began to *enjoy* them, but began eating them much more frequently, abandoning processed, often horrendously expensive, snacks and substitutes that I had eaten in the past. In other words, my daily consumption of fresh fruits and vegetables went from about 10 percent of my total daily food intake to over 70 percent in a short period of time. If you add in my favorite fruit: wine, then it's closer to ninety. It is thus easy to see how your savings from growing much of your own food can be far greater than you might at first think.

How much can we save as a society by bringing back the old victory garden? Well, for a start, we North Americans, who have elevated weight reduction to *the* national pastime, could save most of the $35 billion a year spent on diet programs and liposuction alone. Consider how much additionally could be saved in hospital bills for curing all the ailments caused by the eating of fats and junk foods, everything from diabetes, heart disease, and stroke to various cancers.

Thus, by switching to a much healthier diet—everyone from the National Academy of Sciences to the American Cancer Society recommends a high-fiber, low-fat one—which you tend to get when you grow your own food, the financial gains nationally could be almost endless.

Eating well

> "We are living in a world today where lemonade
> is made from artificial flavors and furniture
> polish is made from real lemons."
>
> —ALFRED E. NEUMAN

If you tried, by and large, to eat only what you grew, then you would have to say goodbye to Quarter-Pounders, Diet Coke, sugar Pops and Twinkies. What a blessing! The first week you might miss them; the second you will not believe you had ever insulted your taste buds and innards by ingesting such obscenities.

When was the last time you ate a real tomato? I don't mean the red watery kind; I mean one that explodes with a hundred flavors as you take a bite. If you haven't for a long time then that's sad, but what is even sadder is that while some of us can at least *remember* a real tomato, most of our children have grown up eating only imitations. And worse than not being able to eat the tomato we once loved is never having eaten a real tomato at all.

But how can we account for such a great difference in flavor?

FIRST, IT IS estimated that more than half of all tomatoes—and many fruits—consumed in the US, are harvested and shipped green, and then artificially ripened with chemicals or radiation upon arrival at their final destination. No comparison in flavor with those ripened on the vine. Allow me to tell you something I learned from twelve years of working our vineyards.

Our grapes turn a dark color; i.e. *look* good and ripe, sometime in early August. Do we pick them? Over my dead body. We wait. We wait all of August and some of September before I even begin testing the ripeness of our earliest maturing grapes: our Syrah. When the leaves start to yellow and the stem near the cluster has turned woody and brown (both signs that the vine is becoming dormant); when the seeds too have turned brown and taste toasted-sweet instead of bitter; when the color of the skin stains your lips, teeth and fingers; when the refractometer, which indicates sugar levels, reads a "perfect" 24, *then* the grape is ripe. That's the time when I prepare for the harvest and—you guessed it—wait some more. I don't know the chemistry of the why, but I know that with an extra week of maturation the perfumes and flavors take on a new intensity that simply was not there before. I do the same with the Sangiovese grapes for our Brunello. The results? Our Syrah was named Italian Red of the Year in New York, and our 2006 Brunello, just released, received 95 points from James Suckling who has thirty years of experience tasting for *Wine Spectator*.

Somehow, I don't think we would have done so well had we picked the grapes early and "matured" them in a box with cyanide or a nuclear blast or whatever it is the "maturing" industry uses.

SECOND, WE HAVE to realize that in a culture obsessed with looks, fruits and vegetables are no longer grown for flavor but for appearance. Most of us don't shop at farmers' markets where we are enticed by the vendor's cries to sample his sweetest, ripest or juiciest, but in supermarkets, where if we bit into an apple we would be arrested for unauthorized mastication. We are, in other words, expected to judge what we eat by looks alone.

THEN THERE IS the question of purity. About 500 million pounds of pesticides and herbicides a year are poured on what we eat. True, some of these toxins leach out, but some end up on our plates. Most of them have only one purpose: to make agro-businesses more profitable. In others words, if you grew your own food you could exclude these toxic delicacies from your menu.

But the above toxins used in growing are only a beginning. Next is the processing. Apart from genetically modified food, we have the above mentioned artificial ripening either with chemicals or by radiation (have you ever checked to see if you glow in the dark?) plus a slew of antibiotics, preservatives, correctives, additives and food dyes. To describe their individual or combined dangers would fill volumes. The important point is that all of this ingestion of who knows what—not to mention salmonella and e-coli, distant food poisonings by oil-spills and even nuclear contamination—can be avoided if you grow your own.

Some may shrug at this and say, "So what's a little pesticide, preservatives and a bit of poisoning? And so what if things don't taste as good as they could?" But it is not as simple as that. Apart from the health hazards of agro-food-chemicals there's another factor. The flavor of the vegetables and fruits we eat is not merely luxury. It is just as connected to our lives and the world around us as the air we breathe or the water we drink. If we do not learn about, if we are not exposed to, the hundreds of unique flavors our fruits and vegetables can provide, then we will never learn to love them. In the same way, if we have never seen or smelled the clear blue sky of a

winter prairie or a summer mountain, we will unques-
tioningly accept our filthy city air. If we don't know the
thrill of a forest, we will learn to accept our moribund,
concrete cities. That is why we should fight tooth and
nail for a real tomato; full of flavor, full of sun.

The Environment

"Year by year, the energy cost of each mouthful of
our food has increased, until now we are using about ten
times as much energy as our meals contain."

—ROGER B. SWAIN

Lest we forget, or never think of at all, the way we cultivate, transport, process, package and market our foods
results in staggering quantities of avoidable pollution.

Farming is no longer farming, it is agro-industry
based on agro-chemicals. These agro-chemicals pollute
not only our bodies, but cause vast collateral damage
during their manufacture and application, and "increase
health risks to agricultural workers, harm wildlife, and
pollute groundwater."

Then, of course, there is the great god of modern
times: transportation. The average food in North America
travels a staggering *eleven-hundred miles*. In your back
yard it would average about eleven steps. A Worldwatch
Institute report warns of devastated economies and

unlivable environments if we continue to mass-produce and mass-transport food. In a sustainable world, where carbon emissions must be cut by two-thirds, we "cannot be trucking vast quantities of food thousands of miles."

But the amount of pollution saved from eliminating transport pales in comparison to the pollution caused by food processing, packaging, and marketing. To be specific: the farmer receives on average only 25 cents of each dollar you spend on food. The other 75 cents go to . . . ? Exactly.

Eating only food you grow would limit you to eating what is in season. Is that so bad? Do we have to eat strawberries in November or watermelons in January? Can we not build our excitement as we do for Thanksgiving and Christmas? Do we have to have everything all the time? How dull. As Goethe said, "Nothing is harder to bear than a succession of fair days."

Social and Personal

Even not counting the above three factors, social bonds— whether within the family or with neighbors—and the personal benefits that a food garden can bring, is enough justification for us to go and dig.

Spending most of our lives nearly as inert as a corpse—apart from our twitching fingers on joysticks and keyboards—we have become so unaccustomed to even walking that to call our current lurch a "waddle" would be an insult to a duck. Hence the robust actions of working the soil will feel like a return to Eden for our bodies. The complex movements of constant stretching, bending, twisting, swinging and hauling, all those barely noticeable movements you do while in your garden, are both physically and emotionally rewarding. Candace hasn't been in a gym in her life. She just turned sixty and hates exercise. All she does is look after our fruits and vegetables; the rest of the garden she never touches, and she has firm hard muscles and weighs exactly as much as when she was twenty: a hundred and six pounds on a five-foot six-inch frame. The benefits of such work do not end when we step out of the garden; they continue to give a zest and limberness to our daily lives. They remind us that we are a mobile species designed and built to make miraculous motions: to run and jump, spin and dance. Working a garden lets us regain one of life's greatest joys: the joy of movement.

When we work our gardens with others—family, friends, lovers—those movements take on a yet more special meaning: we move together. There is a kind of exhilaration when working with someone in close quarters: taking care how we swing our hoe without doing them harm, making sure we don't leave a rake where the other can trip over it—seeming stupidities—but when we have to think about allowing others a space to move, when we anticipate their moves, and blend our moves with theirs, it's a kind of basic choreography; a kind of primordial dance.

The importance of this is not in the artistic or aesthetic, but in the profoundly human: we share. We learn the beauty of working together, of achieving results together we could not have reached alone. We learn the joy of community.

THEN THERE IS the joy of knowing a physical skill. To be a child and discover—or be older and re-discover—that we are actually capable of doing things with our hands other than opening the car door, or combing our hair, is a confidence builder *sans pareil.* Producing something through physical work, furnishes us with a basic confidence: we can take care of ourselves.

Within the family, working together outdoors then preparing and celebrating a feast, will create not only a lasting tie, but can give your children a secure emotional foundation for life.

Ofelio's granddaughter Celeste, who just turned four, lives with her mother, father and older brother in a house next to her grandparents' and uncle's. She is an enthusiastic worker in the garden with her grandpa. But that's just the beginning. After they carry the fresh food into the kitchen, Celeste helps her grandma and aunt prepare the daily meals.

Now Celeste is no isolated farm child, she "updates" her Facebook page, and dresses to the teeth. Last time we went for dinner, she rushed off as we arrived yelling, "*Arrivo subito. Devo trucarmi!*" I'll be right back; have to do my make-up. And back she came, lipstick eye shadow, dark-nails, and all. But she didn't settle into the role of little princess. She bustled about, bringing in the food, checking to make sure everyone had everything (there were fifteen of us at the table), then as soon as a course was done, she was off changing plates, bringing wine and more food. This was her grandpa's house where she was not only madly loved, but where she fit in and was needed.

WHEN WE LANDED in Canada we had but our clothes in one small suitcase and a hundred or so dollars my parents had saved by working the winter and spring in Vienna. We lived near Vancouver in a three-room attic with a view of the mountains and a mandarin orange crate hung out the window for a fridge. But we immediately found a treasure in my stepfather's great uncle, Feribacsi. He had a place nearby that, even in retrospect, seems like paradise to me. His valley had once been full of small farms, and across the road a chicken farm still lingered, where you could take your battered egg carton and come back with it full of eggs, some still warm, some still with bits of straw sticking to the shell. Feribacsi lived with his wife, Ildiko, in a small, one-bedroom house, perfectly kept and surrounded by vegetables and flowers, but it was the two acres of land behind the house that I really loved. There, beyond an orchard and an overgrown field, were the woods and, in them, an abandoned chicken coop.

Many years before there must have been a clearing behind the coop, because there were no trees there, only waves of brambles washing over the roof and pouring in through the windows. One spring evening, Feribacsi announced that if we wanted to have our own vegetable garden, the bramble jungle behind the chicken coop was ours.

We started hacking on a Sunday morning, my stepfather in the lead wielding a machete, my mother behind him tugging brambles with a rake, and me bringing up the rear with an army shovel, whacking away at berry roots that grew all the way to China. We must have looked laughable; three city slickers who had never touched a tool bigger than a tooth-brush in their lives. Every evening after work, we picked up our weapons, and attacked. It was May. The northern evenings were long. There was still light in the sky as we walked home to our attic, tired as dogs but in stitches at my attempts at yodeling like Gene Autry. We slept well. We survived two weeks of hacking, sweating, and yodeling to clear that patch of dirt. Then we turned the soil. My God what soil it was. I was only eleven and knew nothing about humus or fertility, but there was something about that thick, black forest loam, the way it crumbled in your hand, the way its fragrance filled the air.

We laid out the plant beds straight and even, each as wide as the pick handle was long, then we stomped down the paths to keep the weeds from growing, and then, on the tenth of June, three months to the day after we set foot in the New World, we seeded the black soil of our piece of land.

For a week, we watered the barren soil each night, then walked home. I never said a word, but I had great doubts that anything would ever emerge from that empty dirt. Then one Saturday it happened. It was hot. The sun was high, the sky clear, and by late afternoon the cedar trees around us gave off a sweet fragrance I had never smelled before. I was near the garage helping Feribacsi wash his maroon 1954 Ford, preparing it for the Sunday drive, when a joyous cry from the chicken coop cut the air. We ran. My stepdad and my mom were leaning over the seeded beds, calling "Look, look!" I squatted by the beds and tilted my head sideways and saw, in the barren earth, lit by the sinking sun, standing in rows like miniature solders, delicate green shoots reaching toward the sky.

It was a good summer. Dennis Mitchell and I made a fort in a hollowed stump, and in the evenings we watered and weeded our garden. By August it was lush with radishes and parsley and celery and onions; on Sundays, we went fishing in that shallow muddy creek, and to the relief of the whole family, I completely and forever lost my urge to yodel.

Throughout that fall we were back behind the chicken coop, loading up on fresh corn, and green and yellow peppers, some of them so spicy they brought tears to our eyes, and parsnip and carrots and potatoes, or just sitting on the coop's steps, still warm from the sun. And even on October evenings, when the northern winter reared its frosty head, that garden kept us together not behind the coop but in the attic kitchen. We canned.

That piece of earth had provided food to last us through the winter. We spent the evenings gutting peppers, shredding cabbage to be pickled, slicing beets to be boiled, peeling little onions and stuffing them in Mason jars. We built shelves in the low part of the attic, where it was coolest, to house the rows of jars full of more colors and flavors than you can name. And through the winter months the garden remained with us. It was there at dinner each time a jar was opened with a pop, each time we crunched a pickle. It was there as clear as a summer's day with, "Remember that damned shovel," or "that huge melon" or "that slug." It was there through the muddy spring on the cleaned-off kitchen table with the colored bags of seeds and carefully penciled plans of the beds, with so much designated for this, so much for that.

Vegetable gardens held the family together for years, behind the coop, then behind our tiny house, then later behind the big house we built on a hill. But with each place, with each year it grew a little smaller, and with each place, with each year we grew slowly apart. The only meals we shared those last years were on holidays, and there was just a row of parsley left the year my mother died.

Whether abandonment of the garden was a cause of the rift between us, or a symptom, who can say. But in those gardens there were special moments: a lot of good ones and probably more bad than I remember, but whatever else those gardens gave us, they gave us common ground. My mother had her own job and my stepfather had his, and I had school and sports and friends, and we all had our own problems, needs, dreams and fears, but in that garden we shared and shared alike, loved it and hated it, weeded, worried, and harvested all together. Perhaps that's not much, but in a world as chaotic as ours, where ties between us loosened long ago, isolating parents, estranging children, and giving us so little common ground to share, then, at least looking back, that garden seems an island remote from senseless struggles, where not only could we shut the world out, but we could shut ourselves in—alone but together.

CHAPTER 11

Financial Obesity

THE 1970S WERE still an age of moderation, exemplified by the fact that for New York lawyers and teachers, starting salaries were about the same. In those days, the number of overweight or obese in the populace hovered around 10 percent. But by 2010, the U. S. Department of Health and Human Services classified 66 percent of adults in the United States as overweight or obese. That same year, the starting salaries for NYC lawyers had ballooned to *four times* that of the city's teachers. The DHHS goes on to point out the dangers of physical obesity as, "increased risk for chronic diseases such as heart disease, type 2 diabetes, high blood pressure, stroke, and some forms of cancer."

The explosion of body mass has been blamed on everything from constant snacking, to junk food, to consumption of huge portions, and more and more on emotional disorders. At last, the question is being asked, "Why are we compulsively snacking? Why do we binge on junk food? And why do we eat such huge portions?"

Overeating has been associated with depression, boredom, loneliness, anxiety, frustration, stress, problems with interpersonal relationships and poor self-esteem.

The cause and effect is illuminated in an article from Britain's National Health Service. It starts with an insightful quotation. "I have just finished with my boyfriend and now I'm eating chocolate. I know it's not chocolate that I want. I want a kiss and a cuddle. I want *him*. So why am I trying to find solace within that sheet of silver foil?"

According to Professor Andrew Hill, a psychologist at Leeds University, that is precisely the question we should be asking if we want to understand overeating. To him the simpleminded approach to curbing obesity—by counting how many calories we consume and how many we burn—is guaranteed to fail. "There's energy in and there's energy out but there's a person in-between," he says. "You need to understand the emotional reasons for eating if you are ever going to change behavior."

He points out that from infancy, food is directly linked to emotions: the breast not only feeds, but comforts; favorite foods are used to calm and reward. Sweets forever remind us of the sweetness of mother's milk. This changes little as we grow older. "What does a man give a woman when he is wooing her? Chocolates. What do you give your family for a special occasion? You take them out for a meal or you make a special meal."

It is then safe to say that overeating is not about filling empty stomachs, it's about "a kiss and a cuddle"—it's about filling empty arms.

THE REAL PROBLEM is not what we are doing, but what we are *not* doing, while we're doing what we do. While food becomes a fleeting substitute for someone's loving arms, it unfortunately gets us no closer to what we really need. On the contrary. Overeating sets a vicious cycle in motion: the more weight we gain, the more self-conscious we become, and the more reluctant to go out and meet someone to love. So we become even more lonely, anxious, frustrated and depressed. And, to feel better, we eat even more.

WHILE OUR SOCIETY is understandably focused on the unhealthy effects of plain to the naked eye physical obesity, few have questioned a less obvious, but more disturbing disorder affecting not only those suffering from it, but demoralizing and dehumanizing us all. Significantly enough, this disease began to go viral at about the same time as did physical obesity, and quickly became a pandemic infecting the whole world. Its symptoms are similar—swelling and ballooning—but instead of hips and thighs, it's of bank accounts. This disorder could be termed, without malice, "financial obesity."

While overeating can be understood, it is less clear what voids over-earners try to fill. In other words, what drives someone to accumulate wealth beyond any possible use or need? What motivates millionaires and billionaires to work nearly night and day, with no concern for friends, family or society, focusing on some menial endeavor that most often involves nothing more mentally challenging than buying and selling with the single-minded purpose of accumulating *more*? Were this kind of behavior exhibited by another species—like our dog, say we found it running endlessly around the neighborhood pilfering a dog biscuit here, another there, then piling them sky high in quantities that he couldn't eat were he to live to be a hundred—would we not, in a panic, rush to call the vet?

When looking for the "why" of over-earning, I think we have to dismiss comparison to eating disorder motivations—of trying to relive the sweetness of mother's milk and her comforting breast, for few people I know were brought up snuggling Rolex watches or sucking hundred dollar bills.

While physical obesity results in damage to our arteries, liver and heart, it is more difficult to measure financial obesity's damage to the organ it affects most: our brain. It's fair to say that the vital neurological paths—

those formed by frequent use, as we'll examine in chapter 14—would be of the most limited kind, made up primarily of basic arithmetic: figuring gain and loss. Most other vital paths—curiosity, imagination, warmth, kindness and empathy—had they ever developed, would have all atrophied, from disuse, long ago. I think we can assume that, as every other human, the financially obese need "a kiss and a cuddle." Lacking the qualities which are normally inviting—warmth, kindness, imagination—they continue to substitute with an inanimate satisfaction, one they can count, and count on—money.

The point of this discussion is a simple one: Since the explosion of financial obesity corresponds in time to the explosion of physical obesity, there must be some aberration in our recent culture that has caused them both. In other words, we can assume that the emotional problems—depression, boredom, loneliness, anxiety, frustration, stress, problems with interpersonal relationships and poor self-esteem—that lie behind over-gorging are the same whether the over-gorging out is of the physical or financial kind.

What, you may ask, has this to do with real life? Well, since most cases of obesity are caused by emotional disorders which we feel obligated to address and treat to save the patient, then are we not equally if not more obligated to identify and treat the emotional problems of the financially obese? Not just out of fairness but out of self-preservation. Decades of obsessive hoarding and unbridled greed have led directly to a near economic collapse; hence the emotional disorders of the financially obese affect not only *them* but have severe repercussions on the welfare of us all.

The first step is obvious: to recognize financial obesity for what it is—a runaway pandemic. Second, instead of admiring it and refusing to see its danger, treat it like any other emotional problem or mental disease: with attentive understanding and care.

AND MAKE SURE we "kiss and cuddle" a hell of a lot more.

CHAPTER 12

Mortgage, Sweet Mortgage

IN THE PAST thirty years, while the size of the average family has decreased, the size of the average North American home has nearly doubled from 1,200 to over to 2,000 square feet. Why?

A FRIEND SENT me a clipping this summer from *The Washington Post*, entitled "Trading life on land for love of family." It chronicled the story of the Crafton family who, when the children were 8, 11, and 15, set out in a 43-foot sailboat for a seven year circumnavigation of the globe. Kathy and Tom Crafton had successful careers; she was an ICU nurse, he a psychologist. They had status, the big house, and everything material they could want. They yearned for only one thing: more time together. One day they looked at each other and said, "What the hell are we doing?" They quit their jobs, sold the big house and moved onto the boat whose interior is not much larger than a hefty pick-up camper. Yet, Tom remembers, that the day they moved aboard, "Sibling rivalry stopped. We just seemed to get along better the longer we were out there."

They sailed the Americas for two years then set out for the South Pacific. They stayed for three months in Vanuatu, one of their favorite places where "people owned the least and smiled the most. They are the happiest people in the world. It reinforced everything we believed in about putting in time with the family over this blind pursuit of material things."

For seven years they sailed the world and even now, on the boat back in Maryland, they make a point of gathering to watch the sunset together, and of getting up early to see it rise.

The article concludes with a comment by the now 18-year-old Kali, friendly, freckled and smiley. After spending most every night of the past seven years sharing a V-berth in the bow compartment with her sister, last week Kali spent her first night ashore in her grandparents' air-conditioned guest room. It was very still, very roomy and very lonely.

"I missed the boat," she says. "I missed being with everyone."

I know one family's experience may not express a universal yearning, but then again maybe it does.

Ten years after Candace and I met, we hand-built a house on a beach at the bottom of a cliff. It had to be four-stories high with a foot-bridge from the fourth-floor so we could reach the driveway. It was glorious—all glass and cedar with the ocean in front and the cliff behind— three thousand square feet of architectural splendor that felt about as cozy as the Houston Astrodome. After a year of shouting at each other from one empty floor to the next, we rented it out and moved to Paris into a tiny, old flat, where we felt comfortingly near each other; where we felt at home.

Why do we do this to ourselves? Why do we build huge barns when all we *really* want is the security of four walls and the warmth of another soul? Why can't we have the insight of the Crafton family? Or do we want the big house just to impress strangers, to make some poor passerby feel bad for a moment?

It seems that just as we have lost sight of what was special about Sundays—friendships, solitude, calm—so we have lost sight of what was special about home. family, security and peace. And just as Sundays have become not a day of rest, but a day to drag out and service all our gear, so our houses are no longer places that protect us, but instead we protect them, maintaining, paying off, and repairing.

WE NOW LIVE with our son Peter (a.k.a. Buster) in a thirteenth century friary that we restored from a ruin nearly fifteen years ago. It was one of the smallest Tuscan farmhouses we could find as most of them housed, not only four generations, but, also distant relatives, from great aunts to second cousins, plus a wine cellar, granary, and stables that occupied the ground floor.

Now with the house redone—built around a court-yard and an old guard tower—the three of us live *and* work in but a third of it: five small rooms. Candace runs the winery from one, I work in the tower, we sleep in two bedrooms, are seldom in the library but *always* the kitchen. Even though it's no more than 10 by 12 feet, with one long counter with a stove, sink and a small fridge built into a brick nook at the end, with its fire-place aglow from October to April, and an old wooden table with four chairs, *this* is the heart of the house. We cook and eat two full meals a day there, gossip and argue and laugh until the wine bottle is empty. Candace reads there in the evenings by the fireplace, and we play chess or poker on long winter nights. When friends and neigh-bors drop in, that is where we sit and sip wine, and in the wee hours when all is still, that's where I go to write.

When dear friends come for long stays, even though there's a sizeable old dining table in the next room, they all prefer to squeeze around the kitchen table, to be close not only to the warmth of the fire, but to be close to each other, to be close to us. We often crowd six or seven, elbow-to-elbow, around a table meant for four, for din-ners that start at eight and last through bottles of wine. The rest of the house remains dark and empty.

In the winter, we close off all but the rooms where we stay; if one day the empty half of the house crumbled, we might not even notice.

So why do we suffer from McMansion madness? Why do we build a multitude of rooms each with a giant screen where we hide away in a futile attempt to forget our loneliness? Perhaps if we all had a small old kitchen table, we might learn again to enjoy each other. And we might again fill the night with good conversation that sharpens our wit, teaches us to listen, and teaches us that someone else might have another point of view.

The Modern Kitchen as a Symptom

Our kitchens are living proof of how society has changed. The new kitchen is as big as a whole house once was; with islands and peninsulas, they resemble small nations. We have refrigerators so large they are the envy of a morgue, dishwashers and garburators, garbage compactors, microwaves and convection ranges, barbecue grills, and a dozen machines that slice, dice, whirl and whack; marble slabs for this, stainless slabs for that. The only thing our kitchens lack is a place for people.

Why?

The explanation seems simple: in a society where we, who live in the house, almost never have a say in its building or design, the only determinant to how it's built is *profit*. As Steven Jobs, the world's gadget-god said blithely not long ago, "It's not the consumer's job to know what they want."

No. The consumer's job is to obediently gobble up whatever some huckster puts before him. That is what leads to a booming economy. Until it crashes.

WE NO LONGER have master craftsmen to thoughtfully build us a house to suit our needs; how big or how small; whether we'd like it with an enclosed courtyard, or a backyard or without; how big to make our rooms, how many or how private; or whether we prefer to use logs or stones or mud. Instead all decisions rest in the hands of "developers," who, in the blink-of-an-eye bulldoze a hundred acre meadow, or orange grove, or desert, and mass-produce a thousand identical, matchstick houses, in which, if you're lucky, you get to choose the color of the rugs.

So, the bigger the house—and the more gear that's packed in it—the more can be charged for it; hence the greater the profit.

There's very little profit in a small kitchen with a table.

How big is big enough?

Let's start comfortably, but sensibly right from the entrance. It should have a bench where we can sit and take off our shoes and a closet to keep our coats in, let's say 6 by 8 feet, or about 50 square feet.

If you agree with me that our kitchen with a fireplace, a brick bread oven, a marble counter, table and bench is functionally sufficient, then add 125 square feet—not bad for the place where we cook, eat, and loiter. To be on the safe side, let's tack-on a walk-in pantry to stock for the winter, say 5 by 5 feet, so that's another 25 square feet.

A living room should be spacious enough to accommodate friends and relations but not so big that you need to call a cab to cross it. Fifteen feet by 15 feet is plenty for a fireplace, a couch, two armchairs, bookshelves, and an upright piano. Size: 225 square feet. Believe it or not, we have so far used up a total of only 425 square feet.

Let's build a couple of bedrooms, each 12 by 12 foot, two 8 by 8 foot bath rooms, and another room-worth for storage and we have a *sub* total of 516 square feet for a grand total of 941. So let's add another small room, and we have a cozy home of 1,000 square feet. Now what on earth does the modern family do with the average house that's twice as big? Bowl? Square dance? Drag race in the hall?

Not only would a functional 1,000 square foot house cost a pittance to build, but you could build it with your nearest and dearest easily in a year, with nice long lunch breaks and a pause now and then for the occasional scuffle. And just think, with space saved, how wonderfully large your yard would then be—room for a veggie garden for the kids to play, for you to futz around or hangout with your neighbors, and for the turtle to go wild.

Now many will ask, "But where is the garage?" I'd have to answer humbly, "Nowhere." I mean really; cars are driven on roads and freeways most of which have no roof, and most are parked all day under open skies, so why do they need to be tucked in for the night? Would they whimper with fear if left out in the dark?

I won't go into the other misguided parts of our houses that we now seem to feel to be as vital as our organs: the cathedral entrance where no one prays, the vast dining room where no one dines, the family room that has seldom seen the family, or the entertainment room where everybody's bored. It should be enough to note that the flashy and useless has now come to dominate most aspects of our lives from junk food with no nutritional value, to the finance industry which adds almost nothing to society except the occasional thrill of near collapse, to our tacky, enormous houses that make us isolated and lonely, and make us shiver with dread of having to pay the *mortgage.*

Which brings us to my favorite topic. So let's take a break from the design of our houses to have a few laughs of the financial kind. Hang on to your hat—after your house is foreclosed, it might just be the only roof you have left.

The Mortgage

One of the cornerstones of the American Dream has been to own a home, and such is our culture of euphemism, that we are lulled into believing that once we sign the mortgage we actually *do*. Well we don't. At best we own but a tiny portion. At worst all we own is a hell of a big debt.

How did this strange state of affairs begin?

Not so long ago, when you came of age and got ready to marry, you went to the end of the village, got the next piece of land, and with the help of your lover, friends and fellow villagers, built yourself a house to shelter you and yours. And that was that. Your house was yours. You could get on with your life, grow and raise what you could, help others when you could, get by, live in peace.

Not any more. Why? Because the land is *gone*. It no longer belongs to your fellow villagers to give, but to the We-Laff-U-Cry Development Corporation headquartered in Shanghai or Dubai or the Moon, and while they won't stop by and help you build your little house, they will happily build a gargantuan one for you, as gargantuan as the bylaws allow. All you need to do is sign the mortgage, the repaying of which will take you all of your life.

What will be a big surprise is just how much you'll repay.

Let's pretend that your new home costs only $100,000—the US average in 2010 was $280,000. And let's say your 30-year mortgage is fixed at 5 percent. Now, let's say you made no down payment and were willing to pay $500 per month or $6,000 per year. Since the interest gets added back onto the principal at the end of every year, the principal goes down very slowly. The mortgage payments would then look like this: first year payment $6,000; interest $5,000; you still owe $99,000. If that leaves you gagging, just look up ahead: 10th year payment $6,000; interest $4,448; *and* you still owe about $89,000.

So, after ten years you have paid the bank a total of $60,000 on your $100,000 mortgage, and you still owe them almost $90,000. Get it? Of course you don't. But then that's the whole idea because the CEOs of banks could never pocket $100 million a year *each* if you did.

If you think I'm lying you can check my calculations by using the following method which I found in my research.

The polynomial appearing before the fixed monthly payment c (with $x = 1 + r$) is called a cyclotomic polynomial; it has a simple closed-form expression obtained from observing that $xpN(x) - pN(x) = xN - 1$ because

all but the first and last terms in this difference cancel each other out. Therefore, solving for $pN(x)$ yields
the much simpler closed-form expression: $pN(x) =$
$1+x+x2+ \ldots .xN-1 = xN-1/ x-1$

If you can stop twitching and frothing for a minute,
I'll give you a more realistic example. If you borrow
$250,000 to buy one of the average $280,000 new homes
at a 7 percent annual interest rate and pay the loan back
over thirty years, then, adding in $1,500 annual property
insurance, and 5 percent annual private mortgage insurance payment, your monthly payment would be about
$2,000. Since over the thirty years you will be making
this donation to Mr. CEO's private yacht/jet/island/
continent a total of three hundred and sixty times, you
can readily see that your $250,000 baby will end up costing you (with your $30,000 down-payment) a whopping
$750,000. Now if that doesn't make you want to dangle
Mr. CEO from a lamppost, I don't know what does. I
mean has anyone looked up the word "usury" lately?

But that's the good news. The bad news is that since
you have to factor in another $pN(x) = 1+x+x2+ \ldots .xN-1$
$= xN-1/ x-1$ to cover heat, maintenance, new shag rug
and lights, you will see that over the 30 years you will
have coughed up around $1,000,000 just so you wouldn't
sleep in a log cabin, stone cottage, or yurt of your own
making or, simpler still, in a hammock under the tropi

cal stars. Now, of course, you could scoff and say, "Yes. But after thirty years the value of my house will have gone up," but then I would reply that judging by the last four years, the new *Up* is *Down*.

SO THERE YOU have it. Remarkable, don't you think? Remarkable that we will have slaved away at some mostly unremarkable job for over thirty years, paying off the mortgage on some thrown together two-by-fours, plaster board, and cheapo plastic siding, that any two of us could have built much better in six months doing enjoyable, commonsense, and totally rewarding work like planning, measuring, sawing, and banging nails.

Of course that would make for a much more simple life, one that has no place for Mr. CEO.

AFTER LIVING TOGETHER for six months, Candace and I built a small house, just the two of us. It was cedar, inside and out, had decks, skylights, oak-floors, a fireplace—all the comforts of home. Its size was a humble 500 square feet, but it had a living room, dining room, study, a fully equipped maple and stainless steel kitchen, a bathroom, and an airy loft bedroom with a deck.

We built the whole thing in three months and it could have been even less had we not made the design so modularly complex, hauled the material in a beat up old Porsche, and built in Vancouver's endless winter rain.

Nevertheless, three months sufficed despite our minimal previous experience, and the house turned out nice enough to be written up in magazines. The cost was—appliances and rugs included—$3000. Now granted this was in 1973, so to allow for inflation let's multiply by four and get $12,000; then add 50 percent to the size so you can comfily swing the cat, $18,000; then throw in a bit of extras to come up with the nice round total of $20,000. And to build the now bigger house at a most leisurely pace, let's quadruple the time to a year.

Now compare this handmade house to the one you bought for a million and we have a difference of $980,000. As for time, a $20,000 mortgage paid back at the same rate as the 30-year mortgage on the big one would take one year. Add this to the year it took to build, and you have a total of two years of work to own a sweet little home. Whichever way you cut it, between the two houses, there is a whopping difference not only of nearly a million dollars but more importantly of twenty-eight hardworking, long years. So no matter how forgiving a Christian you are, you have to admit that, with the million dollar barn, someone has picked your pocket of the best years of your life.

But where is the difference really? First of all I have to add that the house Candace and I built was a houseboat built on pontoons which had cost $500, considerably less than the average lot. And herein lies half the mystery of the million dollar price, since a broad rule of thumb says that about half the cost of a new home is the lot. Now could someone explain to me how a piece of land that's too small to feed a goat can be worth 15 years of a human being's life? The accepted response is that the price is high because this is a popular location, close to planes, trains, and malls, but all that says is that it's a handy place from which to pay the mortgage.

You will immediately protest, saying that you do a lot more than just pay the mortgage: go out to dinner, take in a ballgame, pop in at the gym. True enough. But you do these things for a miniscule portion of the time to add some variety to a mortgage-paying life.

But back to the lot. So society's consensus of "location, location, location," has decided on land value. As we know, land value is not decided by a democratic vote; it is established by a teeny-weeny minority with a mountain of extra cash—current US figures show that 1 percent of the population owns as much wealth as the bottom 90 percent. These over-cashed investors keep bidding up the price of land hence the price of houses. This is called "land speculation." In a civilized society, utilizing surplus cash to drive the price of homes out of an average person's reach (or to enable him to reach it only with the help of a usurious mortgage) would be pooh-poohed and discouraged by the use of portable guillotines. Alas, in ours, it is considered a wise investment, and those who excel at it get—instead of their head in a basket—their faces on the covers of magazines.

Besides the speculator, we pay realtors, lawyers, bankers, mortgage brokers, bureaucrats (through fees, taxes, licenses and permits) and of course our friendly insurance man, just in case someone walks across our mortgaged lawn, drops dead, and sues our ass 'til kingdom come.

All this instead of just going to the end of the village, picking up a shovel and saying, "I build here."

You smile and say how simpleminded an interpretation this is because in a complex, civilized society you need all this interference just to keep some order. But you have to admit that our world is *not* complex by nature or because all of us voted to make it so. It is complex because we have allowed greed to convolute it for us. You might also ask, how would a simpler world be a better place?

Well, if, for example, you had built your own house, and had no mortgage looming over you, I think we can assume that you would spend the twenty-eight years you saved, mostly hanging out: fishing, hiking, surfing, knitting, zucchini-planting, and blackberry picking. Not only would all these activities result in much less pollution than your neighbors' long hours at the local steel mill, strip mine, or cadmium company, but you would, with so much time spent close to friends, family and nature, develop a more thoughtful, more fulfilling life.

Even Freud, one of the great fans of "civilization," emphatically stated that, "The liberty of the individual is no gift of civilization. It was greatest before there was any civilization." Amen to that.

As for the social damage this system has caused, note that in 2010 there were over a million home foreclosures—those are people who actually lost their homes—while 6 million more were delinquent on their payments by more than 60 days.

I'm sure we can all imagine the emotional devastation this causes families. But, just as studies on the trauma of job loss showed, the mere *fear* of losing the job can be as emotionally and physically harmful as the actual loss of the job itself, so we can assume that the disorienting fear that most homeowners—or, more correctly, mortgage owners—feel, must go far, far beyond the 6 million. How many millions stay awake at night thinking "there but for the grace of God, go I"?

This is no American Dream. It's a human nightmare.

I think we all agree it's time for a better life.

The Postmodern Cave

Let's try and forget the mortgage and get back to how we live. Freud came up with an intriguing interpretation of our homes. "The dwelling house was a substitute for the mother's womb, the first lodging, for which in all likelihood man still longs, and in which he was safe and felt at ease."

I don't mean to sound retro, but I would say that cavemen had a better grip on what a house should be than we do. Just think: he found a nice hollow in a rock, hung a bearskin across the door so he could scratch himself in private, chucked around a few throw pillows, and *voilà*: a bachelor pad that would make Donald Trump rot with envy. Cost? Diddly squat. And what comfort—sixty-five degrees Fahrenheit summer and winter, no roof to fix, no siding to paint, no pipes to freeze up.

But instead of learning from the caveman and building into the perfectly temperature-controlled ambiance of a hillside or artificial berm, we mindlessly stuck exposed little boxes completely above ground where they could be blistered by the sun; battered by icy winds and weathered on all sides by rain. When someone came along with a thoughtful, inexpensive and practical design like Frank Lloyd Wright's Taliesin West in the 1930s, it was treated as a quaint museum piece and remained exactly that.

Half-buried in the hills of the Sonora desert, Wright plucked the sand, gravel, and stone used as basic construction materials from the mountainside. Much of the house was made of sloping walls of stone. This is an extremely cheap and easy way to build, especially for amateurs, as the stones are set with ample cement, thus requiring little fitting. And being cut into the hill, the house provided the same heating and cooling as a cave.

A hundred wise innovations have come and gone since Taliesin: berm houses built into an artificial mound, sod roofs, heated cement floors, pre-cast concrete walls with built in insulation—and while the rare one has been retained in commercial buildings, our tacky sprawl goes on building flimsy exposed boxes out of sticks. The only construction innovations retained in the past hundred years were plastic siding, shag rugs and AstroTurf. Bravo.

And the problem is that just as junk food leaves no room for nourishing and healthy food, and just as watching TV leaves no time for physical activity or friends, so our shoddy housing leaves no room for what could be structurally meaningful, long-lasting, aesthetic and real—all characteristics which would lead to high quality, environmentally-sound and enduring houses.

And worst, with mass-produced industrial housing there remains no opportunity to use our creativity and imagination to invent something new or to express our own wants and needs.

The House of Gadgets

How simple logic, reasoning and the common good have been left out of our houses, might best be exemplified by the multitude of gadgets in them. Take, for example, the clothes dryer. For millennia we dried our clothes on bushes, fences or lines outside. No more. Now there's a machine that by most estimates consumes 10 percent of all electricity on the continent. To reduce pollution (much of that electricity comes from coal-powered generators) and our dependence on foreign oil, in the latest gold-rush of corporations wanting to cash-in on the Green Movement and its accompanying government subsidies, hundreds of millions of tax-payer funds have been solicited to build giant energy-producing solar power and wind generators covering hundreds of square miles of both land and sea. May I suggest we start with a more humble alternative: the clothesline.

Not only is it a twofer (it uses both wind and sun), has low visual impact when empty (casts an eight-inch wide shadow), would eliminate almost 10 percent of the continent's electricity consumption, but, best of all, it requires no taxpayer subsidies. Indeed the capital investment is $1.99.

Not long ago our backyards were animated with freshly-washed clothes dancing in the breeze, and, even today, around much of the world, laundry day turns cities and the countryside into festooned sights. As much as I love Venice's *palazzi*, canals, and churches—I often escape the bustle of the winery to write there in a friend's attic—my favorite Venetian day is invariably Monday, when the city seems to blossom with long lines of laundry dangling from the windows, crossing above the streets, fluttering in the sunshine. The city feels alive then, seems to have a sense of purpose, a spark.

At our house, the clothesline is stretched between two trees. I enjoy the little break to go and hang the laundry or to take it in; gives me a chance to glance at the hills, the trees, get a breath of fresh air. And it might sound laughable, but compared to writing, the success of which I can seldom be sure of, hanging up the laundry feels like an accomplishment.

And yet in most North American communities, not only is hanging the laundry outside not compulsory— which it should be if we are serious about saving the planet for our children—but hanging laundry outside is actually *banned.* If that is not a sign of insanity, I don't know what is. I mean are clean clothes somehow visually offensive? A dog dragging himself along in convulsions, dumping a steaming load on the sidewalk or our lawn is deemed acceptable but clean clothes on a line are disgusting?

Some may say that the dryer saves a few minutes— which I doubt because hang-dried clothes are easier to iron—but then my question is: a few minutes for what? To catch another game show or soap? To Google the sports scores for the tenth time today? Or to read the gossip column to see what inanity which airhead said to whom? Is that really preferable to standing in the backyard soaking up the sunshine, getting a little air, moving your body, catching up on some gossip with the neighbors over the fence?

THE OTHER MACHINE which is now in the Mom and Apple Pie category is the dishwasher. I know most of you gag at the thought of hand washing dishes, vehemently citing the time it consumes. Think again.

I must admit I have done less than empirical research on this subject, but I did, as is my habit, do our dishes by hand after lunch today, and here are the results. Three pasta-bowls, three plates, three wineglasses (cylindrical, bomb-proof, no stem) three sets of cutlery, three espresso cups, two pots and a frying pan: total wash, dry and put-away time: 11.5 minutes. Now if you say that you and your dishwasher can clean up quicker than that, you're a bigger liar than I thought you were.

At our house, Buster and I usually fight over who gets to do the dishes. We both like doing them. When we do them together, we chat about work in the winery, the ails of the world, or the hilarious lines we heard in some movie we watched the night before. When we do dishes each on his own, he uses the solitude for reflection, and I for my rendition of *Love Letters in The Sand*, something no sane biped would dare perform in the presence of another.

I won't go into details about the hundred other gadgets that turn our kitchens into warehouses of mostly forgotten machines: electric knives, deep fryers, waffle irons, ice-cream makers, choppers, grinders, mashers, squeezers, whippers, snappers, pulpers and slashers: but I can tell by the look on your face that you'd forgotten most of these in the depths of your cupboards long ago.

The sad part is that the kitchen, once the heart and soul of our houses, where friends and family gathered for some unforgettable times, lies mostly as cold and emptyas the rest of our McMansions.

Our Neighbor's Kitchen

When we first moved to Italy in 1987, the farm family next door took us under its wings. (Those of you who have read *The Wisdom of Tuscany* are allowed to turn the page.) The Paoluccis were sustenance farmers; they had a small vineyard, some olive trees, fruit trees, fields of wheat, hay and corn, a few pigs, a handful of cows, uncountable chickens, rabbits and Guinea hens, and a bit of woods that kept their kitchen fireplace ablaze through the winter day and night.

The Italian word *casa* means house but in Tuscany it mostly means the kitchen. The Paoluccis' kitchen was from the seventeenth century (their house has a colorful name *Il Palazzo del Diavolo*) and had high ceilings with huge oak beams from which sausages hung in the winter to get dry and *stagionato*. The thick stonewalls plastered over by hand were whitewashed, the terra-cotta tiles of the floor were all worn round. An enormous fireplace covered half the long wall, its great brick hood supported by stone columns, and, below it, on the raised hearth—inside the fireplace—were two benches where you could sit to be close to the flames.

There was an old marble sink, a wood stove, a smaller gas stove, a couch, some cupboards and shelves. Two old tables stood end-to-end, one with a marble top—ideal for kneading and rolling dough—the other covered with oil cloth.

This kitchen was where the family lived. This was where the youngest daughter Eleonora did her homework; where Carla, her sister, sewed or argued with her boyfriend; where Rosanna, their mother, cooked sauces with great patience, and filled jars with stewed tomatoes or thick wild-plum jam; where Nonna, the grandmother, roasted chicken and stuffed veal in the wood fired oven, and knitted socks and mitts and scarves from raw wool for the family; where Paolucci sat with his craggy hands whittling at a knife-handle or a hoe-handle while he sipped his wine and talked about the animals that he loved, or his grapes or his olives, or the heat or the rain, or joked with his daughters or welcomed his neighbors.

And this was where, twice a day, the family ate its daily meals of pasta or *brodo*, roast meat, salad, cheese, fruit and wine, all of it fresh from right around the house, the vegetables from the garden, the pasta made by hand on the marble table, the meat from the barnyard, olive oil and wine from the cellar below.

So that was the Paoluccis' kitchen. It was also their dining room, their living room, their family room, their media room and the place where they played cards. And as far as I can tell, if they'd built themselves a yawning dining room, a spacious living room, and all those other rooms where most of us sit alone with a machine, they would have gained nothing at all. But they might have just lost something. They might have just lost each other's company. They might have lost someone to yell at, or talk to, or touch, or make them smile out of the blue. They might have stopped being as natural and unself-conscious as you can only be around people you love and trust. They might have forgotten how to be tolerant of each other; they might—little by little—have forgotten how to be a family. They might have, unintentionally, imperceptibly and perhaps irreversibly, grown apart.

CHAPTER 13

How Do You Hug
an Electronic Friend?

I WAS ALMOST twelve when I saw my first TV. After escaping during one long winter night through the hard, snow-packed countryside from communist Hungary, we spent six months in Vienna, then moved to the West Coast of Canada. Arriving at a refugee camp at an abandoned air force base, there it was: a little box in which I could see the whole world.

I was smitten.

Knowing little English never gave me pause; watching things move was good enough. The action was riveting: cowboys on horses, chasing, shooting, singing—one of them even yodeling—tough guy private eyes catching bad guys left and right.

Back in Hungary, I had lived a street life with our local gang, played soccer on the cobblestones with a ball made

of old rags, or played war with a wooden sword my grandfather had carved, or went to the park and built a fort in
the bushes. But in Canada, it was different. My English
was still broken, I was thin and shy, and the games were
weird, like football that you played with your hands, and
baseball that you hit with a stick, and skating on ice. So,
it was easier just to go home, shut the door, and enjoy the
secure company of electronic people on TV.

For the next two years, I was glued to the box. Mickey
Spillane, The Three Stooges, Peter Gunn, Bugs Bunny.
I wrote a letter to Walt Disney's Annette Funicello, and
she sent me an autographed photo. I was in love. It was
a painless love affair. Annette was always there, reliable,
undemanding, big eyes, a little dull but her hair was
always perfect, and then there was her constant, reassuring smile. And she was never cranky; asked for nothing—had to dust her a bit every now and then—and she
never complained, or argued, and even showed up on the
little screen on Sunday.

The love affair ended suddenly when I rediscovered
friends.

After two years, my English had improved, and we
had also moved to a neighborhood full of kids. They
were a pack of tough guys smoking cigarettes, but they
also liked playing impromptu sports, so within a few
weeks I was "in." There was the always joking John
Hardy and the thoughtful Dave Dowsett, quiet Glenn
Dick and loudmouthed Crowder, and the forever cheery

Eddy cruising on his bike. There was no holding me back from that gravelly, weedy schoolyard from the moment school was out until darkness fell.

And what memories. That was all fifty years ago but they still shine brightly; that suitcase-size pool table in the Dowsetts' basement with pitted little clay balls that were anything but round, and those gripping baseball and football games on the school grounds, and playing hockey on the frozen pond in the park, and taking long bike trips to the river to fish, or just sit, or scour old sunken boats for treasures like glass fishing balls, or old nets, or brass nails. There were long days at the beach when we came home lobster red, and hours of making round skimboards out of plywood to glide for what seemed like miles across long pools left behind by the tide. The only TV show we watched was quick and funny, spontaneous and feisty. Like us. It was Laugh-in. The rest of the week the electronic people stayed silent and forgotten in the lifeless box.

IT IS STRANGE how we can slip into a whole way of life without noticing it. In those days we watched TV only when we were sick in bed and couldn't get out to enjoy each other's company. Grownups did much the same. There was even a term for those who couldn't get out much, "shut-ins:" people to be pitied and felt sorry for, the chronically ill or severely disabled. And yet over the years, little by little, television has made "shut-ins" of us all.

According to the A.C. Nielsen Co., the average American watches more than five hours of TV a day. In a sixty-five-year lifespan, that comes to twenty years of waking life staring at the tube.

And if we ever do get out together to be social, TV has wedged itself between us even then, not just in airports and train stations but in restaurants and, that last hold-out of a true community, our bars.

THERE USED TO be another term, this one deprecating, called "geeks." Those were the rare cases of social isolates who preferred their chemistry sets or crystal radios to human company. They were kids in self-exile, perhaps triggered by shyness, perhaps by captivating interests, I really can't be sure, but they grew up with a laser-like focus on toys. They remained mostly introverted, physically awkward, barely communicative, having little care for the world and almost no interest in others. Just as TV has turned most of us into shut-ins, so now computers have turned us into geeks.

A RECENT STUDY by the Kaiser Family Foundation found that kids aged eight to eighteen devote 1,600 minutes per week to watching TV, while the amount of time per week that a child spends in meaningful conversation with his parents is 3 ½ minutes.

When I first read these statistics, I was speechless. It took some time to comprehend that if a child sleeps for eight hours, goes to school for about eight hours, then does "entertainment media" for the rest, his day is over, finished, gone. The frightening question came to mind, that if for half of his waking hours our child is told what to do and think by teachers, and for the remaining half, is told what to do and think by TV "personalities" and video gamesters, then when does the love of our life have time to be him or herself? When does our child have time to be creative or inventive, loving and caring, active and wild—in short: when does our child have time to be a *child?* And since it is mostly these characteristics that distinguish us from turnips, the question arises, when does our child have time to be truly human?

Once we grow older, and our work and commute take up ten hours a day, another two hours we spend doing our chores of shopping, feeding, and cleaning—what Samuel Beckett called, "keeping up premises and appearances,"—five we spend staring brain-dead at the tube, and for the remaining eight we try to get some sleep, then when do we have time—or do we ever—to be ourselves? When do we manage to reflect on our lives, to discuss our dreams and worries with our friends, to exchange ideas, a joke or just a recipe? When do we have time to raise our children, love our dear ones, or just lend a helping hand?

For while it may be true, as so many of us claim, that TV and video games are really "not so bad," their true subtle insidiousness lies in what they replace, what they rob us of: *real* life.

. . .

UNLEASHING TELEVISION ON humanity was like crop-dusting our brains with Valium daily. No aspect of life went untouched: families, friendships, politics, religion, how we worked, what we ate, what we thought, were all permanently altered.

Families that once shared interests and concerns, played some simple card game, or board game together, during which they talked, laughed, expressed their own ideas, now at best share the same TV. At worst they flee separately to their rooms to dissolve in front of their own TV set. Friendships and companionships have been watered down or abandoned. Instead of real flesh-and-blood Eddy next door or the kid down the hall, our pals have become little flashing lights: Annette Funicello, then—God save us—Paris Hilton.

Politicians, who heaven knows were bad enough before, have mutated into TV personalities, whose physical appearance and joviality far outweigh their minds and hearts.

Religion has been changing from quiet contemplation and prayer in humble churches into loud and belligerent ranting on the Tube.

Television turned the world on its head. It was not just the misleading advertising based on the proven notion that you can fool most of the people most of the time, but the programs themselves taught us how much better it is to open a package and slam it into the microwave, or go out and buy a ready-made junk-burger, than to actually use our wits and imagination and create a meal on our own. And TV made the natural world in which we once spent our lives seem inconsequential and dull.

It also changed the way we think about our work. It glorifies and idolizes every single brain-cell occupation from meaty men who kicked, hit, dribbled or drooled, to skinny women with incomprehensible expressions and identically retooled boobs and faces. Thus, if only by sheer exclusion, those doing work of true value to others—the farmer, the craftsman, the fisherman, or the artist who lived a productive, thoughtful life, were relegated to a quaint history.

TV invented a new reality and, without a trace of irony, called it that. And we ate it with a spoon. We actually believed that a handful of people stuck on an island with a TV crew of fifty, and a thousand pounds of food were real Survivors. Up to that point it could be termed a stupid farce, but even worse was the barbarian premise that instead of pulling together as a group, as members of a society whose aim should be the wellbeing of all, the "winner" would be the last one who "survived."

The slew of reality shows that followed were perhaps less vicious but equally unreal and even more embarrassing. People thrown together in resorts or on beaches, where the goal was to destroy an existing relationship, or to form an artificial new one under spotlights with cameras rolling, precluded any genuine human relationship and most emotions except for the occasional outburst of hysteria.

And believing this to be reality, we began to adopt not only their mode of dress, but their emotional responses, moral values and even their thoughtless speech. When kids spend 1,600 minutes a week watching TV and less than 4 minutes talking to their parents, who can blame them for thinking and sounding less and less like live people and more and more like fake "reality" characters. Good thing they were not stuck on the All-Lassie channel or by now they would be barking.

MOST IMPORTANT OF all, television told us that our families and friends are dull, and that our true joy and knowledge come from far away and only from the anointed few. Simple thousand-year-old traditions like storytelling, singing, and even gossiping, that had brought people together and allowed them to learn from each other, to entertain each other, to criticize and discuss, to form friendships and societies, fell by the wayside, replaced by the solitary, numbing, antisocial act of watching TV. As a Mr. Davis, a college educated, amicable New Hampshire farmer, put so well, "Neighbors used to visit every night and talk. But those days are gone. The Tube killed people."

The New York-based Roper Organization's study showed the frightening results. The single activity that most people look forward to daily is not human contact but watching television. Even during dinner, one half of population watches television instead of conversing with family they haven't seen all day. And in times of trouble, we rely on TV to cure us; 35 percent of men said they deal with depression not by talking out or trying to think through their problems, but by watching television. Most heartbreaking of all, when a group of 4 to 6 year olds were given the chance to spend time with their fathers, 54 percent chose to watch TV instead.

Some insist that watching television with others is a social act; compared to watching television by yourself, perhaps. But compared to talking and sharing feelings and ideas, compared to live unrehearsed human companionship, sitting in adjoining chairs watching television is about as socially interactive as squatting in adjoining stalls and dumping into the same sewer. I remember on various occasions having a great time talking and laughing at friends' houses when someone came up with the idea of catching a favorite show. The conversation died, the sharing died, the faces all turned numb. You might as well have dropped a bomb in the room and blown us to the winds, our emotional distance had become so great.

Still others insist that television actually gives us a social foundation; something common to talk about. This is true, but frightening. The bad part is not only that talking about Paris Hilton numbs the brain, but when we talk about these inanities, when we spend our time, thoughts and emotions on distant clowns, we are stealing precious attention and care from our loved ones, or our should-be loved ones—our family and our friends.

It is probably safe to say that the average TV watcher knows more about the love life of his favorite TV bimbo than he knows about his children's, and sadly enough, maybe even cares about it more.

And while our friends and loved ones suffer, we too often stand by idly, but are crushed with heartbreak when we lose Lady Di.

THE SAD PROOF of TV's effect came from an expatriate friend at dinner not long ago. He is in his thirties, witty, pleasant-looking, impeccable education, speaks excellent Italian, yet he lamented about the loneliness of the Tuscan countryside, or more particularly about the difficulty of finding himself a wife. He had been living there for years, fell in with the social circles, both local and expatriate, was always invited to dinners, always circulating, but had remained alone. He told us about how depressed and tired he used to be, until he bought himself a television set. He now no longer feels so "compelled to look," for he can "stay home alone and yet not feel lonely."

This sums up the insidiousness of television: it acts as every other drug or opiate: it deludes us. It makes us feel less lonely by making us believe that the face made out of flickering dots is somehow our friend. Well, it isn't. It's worse than an enemy. If the need really arose, if you really needed someone to make a bowl of soup or wipe a fevered brow, to lend a hand or a shoulder to cry on, or someone to lie beside you and hold you in her arms, the enemy may—overcome by human compassion—turn into a friend or even a lover. But the flickering dots will flicker on uncaring, whether you live or die.

PERHAPS THE GREATEST damage is that without interaction, discussion, or feedback, only the power of presentation, we grow to distrust our own opinion, subjugate our instincts and convictions and actually fool ourselves into believing the most outrageous, self-serving media ravers.

This willingness to accept what we are told, to endow with importance the inane and fake, and most crucial, our willingness to become inactive bystander, watchers, does not end when we turn off the beast. It lingers. We accept that we are helpless, so we become helpless. We lose our natural ability to entertain others and ourselves— a feat most seals and monkeys do with ease— and turn to the Tube. When enough of us are convinced that we are too dull for company, the vast entertainment industry is born. And when, through a lack of human contact, enough of us feel too inadequate to deal with each other, to settle problems face to face, then the vast legal industry is born, and when we don't know how to spend and save, the financial behemoth is born that takes over the world.

And when enough of us convince ourselves that someone else knows better about how the world should work, what is right or wrong, what is to be done, then we will be ready for another a Hitler to lead us.

Yet, we throw our children—at the earliest of ages—to this electronic wolf. What happens then is well described in *The Washington Post*: "Television is the dominant force conveying attitudes and values for the whole of society. Anyone who has ever watched television with a child knows firsthand how frighteningly influential the small screen can be in suggesting not only what to buy but also how to behave and speak and, indeed, what to think."

HOW TV CAN affect children's minds was also reported recently in *Business Week*. "Researchers found that the branding of food product packaging with characters such as Dora the Explorer drives preschoolers to choose higher-calorie, less healthful foods over more nutritious options. The findings, reported online in *Pediatrics*, reflect on the food preferences of 4- to 6-year-old boys and girls who found foods *tastier* when the packaging bore the likenesses of beloved TV and movie characters."

If I was mean-spirited, I would call that brain-washing.

SO WHAT TO do? Turn it off. It's possible.

When Candace did her master's program at The School of Visual Arts in New York, we lived in a tiny studio in Chelsea. I wrote part of the day, the rest of the day I was bored. I went and bought a Sony Trinitron. We hid it in a corner so it would not be too intrusive. Then we turned it on. It felt like an invasion. It felt as if a thousand salesmen had marched in through the door. The TV lasted one night. The next day, I sold the thing and began hanging out in art galleries, museums and bars.

This year, my long-time writing cohort moved with her boyfriend from Brooklyn to Manhattan and decided to skip cable TV. I asked her a few weeks later how life was without TV. "We look at each other more now. We go out more often to see friends and new places," she said. "And we *really* listen to each other."

So turn it off.

After a few days of barely controllable panic, you will not believe how much free time you'll have, what far-ranging thoughts—some utterly antisocial, but very enjoyable—what interests, what great conversations, what calm, and sense of control you will feel. You will have reclaimed your life. You will be free. Free to lead a vibrant, passionate existence, not one broken into tight half-hour segments, three minute advertising breaks, and weekly time slots but your *own* life of wonderfully varied days, new weeks, real seasons, and unforeseeable, ever-changing, surprising lengths of time.

CHAPTER 14

The Shallowing of Our Minds

RECENTLY MY BEST friend ruined my weekend. He grabbed from his shelf a book published last year and said it might fit in with what I was writing. It was titled *The Shallows: What the Internet is Doing to Our Brains.*

I had never read a non-fiction book in two sittings, but Nicholas Carr's book I just could not put down.

He starts off with anecdotal evidence by Bruce Friedman, a pathologist at the University of Michigan Medical School, who notes that since the switch from reading printed material in the form of books to reading books on to the Net a decade ago, he and many of his friends and associates have noticed a marked lack of ability to concentrate. Losing the thread of their thoughts, they are unable to handle not only attention demanding novels like *War and Peace*, but have even "lost the ability to read and absorb a longish article."

Surfing, skimming along the surface of things, taking

"information the way the Net distributes it: in a swiftly moving stream of particles," some of them worry that they have become scatterbrains.

Carr himself notes that, "the Net seems to be chipping away my capacity for concentration and contemplation. I feel like I'm always dragging my wayward brain back to the text. The deep reading that used to come naturally has become a struggle." And he goes on to lament the trend of the "calm, focused, undistracted, linear mind being pushed aside by a new kind of mind that wants and needs to take in and dole out information in short, disjointed, often overlapping bursts—the faster, the better."

He describes the typical new mind as that of a former student body president at Florida State University, a Rhodes scholar, who unabashedly states, "I don't read books . . . it's not a good use of my time . . . I can go to Google and absorb relevant information quickly." And *that* from a philosophy major.

The enormous difference between the two types of reading, Carr describes as follows: "To read a book silently required the ability to concentrate intently over a long period of time, to lose oneself in the pages . . . In the quiet spaces opened up by the prolonged, undistracted reading of a book, people made their own associations, drew their own inferences and analogies, fostered their own ideas. They thought deeply as they read deeply . . .

Quiet, solitary research became a prerequisite for intellectual achievement. Originality of thought and creativity of expression became the hallmarks of the model mind . . . For the last five centuries . . . the linear, literary mind has been the center of art, science and society."

All the above stands in stark contrast to a completely different neuro-involvement, in that, "when we go online, we enter an environment that promotes cursory reading, hurried and distracted thinking and superficial learning." Not to mention superficial thought.

Carr gives no example so I will illustrate his statements with an obvious comparison. The op-ed pages of the print version of *The New York Times* contained, until recently, almost no advertising. You could read without visual distractions about complex often crucial issues like the *Start* treaty, global warming, and the Rwandan genocide, assimilating the articles with what you already knew, filling in spaces with your own opinions, reinforced by sympathy, or even empathy, at the end creating in your mind a brand new and exhaustive bank of knowledge on the topic, a new "complex concept or 'schema'."

No more.

A few days ago I read an op-ed piece on the web-version of *The Times*. The topic was the plight of homeless Haitian children following the earthquake. The piece was not alone on the page. While reading about human suffering, I was invited by a colorful, page-top streamer of smiling faces to "Vote for my Favorite Under 25 Movie star," while being simultaneously coaxed by a fluorescent blue ad to take "A full-body waxing for only $99.95," all the while, a video in a little box ran a trailer for the film *127 Hours* in which someone stuck in a hole decides to saw-off, or chew-off, or nail-file off his own arm.

Was I confused? Not on your life. I recall every detail of how for only $99.95, the Haitian under 25 movie stars got to chew off their own arms last summer at Wax Camp.

Now *that* is what I call power-multitasking.

As for the Haitian children, if they really want my attention, they'll just have to get their own page-top magenta streamer.

THE TREND AWAY from linear reading to the visuals of the electronic screen is truly jaw-dropping. The US Bureau of Labor Statistics for 2008 found young adults between the ages of twenty-five and thirty-four, while putting in 8.5 hrs of screen-time, read only an average of 7 *minutes* a day. To put it bluntly at the risk of over simplifying, that's 510 minutes a day of shallow thinking vs. 7 minutes of linear, *potentially* deep, thought.

Some may shrug and say, So what? Well, as Carr reminded us, the linear, patient mind, "as supple as it is subtle, has been the imaginative mind of the Renaissance, the rational mind of the Enlightenment, the inventive mind of the Industrial Revolution, even the subversive mind of Modernism. It may soon be yesterday's mind."

That prospect frightens me for a truly selfish reason. As you may recall, our childhoods were filled with parents, teachers and elders, advising us to slow down, take our time, think things through, sleep on it, come up with the best all-round solution. I must confess that in my case that had no effect but I'm sure that some of my very favorite people took it to heart. I met two, both doctors, both the directors of their respective departments at Cornell Medical School at New York hospital, one of whom was the "father of sonograms," the other, the world's best in his field. My experience with them after a freak accident ten years ago left me with a complete re-evaluation of the medical profession *and* taught me an unforgettable lesson about life.

One doctor was in his forties, the other in his early sixties, and both had something nearly unearthly about them that in New York City stood out even more: an infinite calm. They translated that into patience and thoroughness, repeating the same procedure, double-checking, triple-checking, rethinking, reconsidering, until they were absolutely satisfied that not a flicker of doubt remained in their minds. They were determined to do the best job with a minimum of interference. Their aim in fact was to avoid any interference at all. And they did. The simplest thing would have been to perform surgery, but they resisted. They reflected. Thought "deeply, linearly, subtly." Thoroughly.

Will the Rhodes Scholar philosophy major, who has no patience for books, bother to do so? Or worse: would he, without the experience of reading and thinking profoundly, even *have developed the ability?*

Piling information atop information, without the wherewithal to have a broad overview; without the ability to consider all sides and all possibilities, without the experience for the kind of thinking we unconsciously develop while reading non-fiction or novels about complicated lives of complex people with often convoluted motivations, without that capacity for "concentration and contemplation," will, I truly believe, lead to a plethora of knee-jerk responses from shallow thinkers, who are conditioned to only superficially "skim" their brains.

It might just result in a society where thoughtless, often senseless outbursts will be the norm because our brains will have been physically transformed.

If I understand neuro-physics, it all works something like this.

Our brain-cells—neurons—are separated from each other by barriers called synapses. The neurons communicate with one another through tentacle-like appendages called axons and dendrites. When a neuron is activated, a pulse releases chemicals called neurotransmitters, which allow the flow of an electric pulse from *its* axon to the dendrite of the *next* nearby neuron setting off a new impulse in that cell which is then, in turn, transmitted to others forming a whole circuit of paths. "Thoughts, memories, emotions," Carr states, "all emerge from the electrochemical interactions of neurons . . . The average neuron makes about a thousand synaptic connections, and some neurons can make a hundred times that number." This varied and unique "mesh of circuits . . . gives rise to what we think, what we feel, who we are.

"As the same experience is repeated, the synaptic links between the neurons grow stronger and more plentiful through both physiological changes, such as the release of higher concentrations of neurotransmitters, and anatomical ones." Either through generation of new neurons, or new terminals on the axons and dendrites, we form "chains of new neurons . . . our mind's true 'vital paths.'"

He quotes the British biologist J. Z. Young, "The cells of our brains literally develop and grow bigger with use, and atrophy and waste away with disuse."

In a brilliantly simplified experiment, biologist Eric Kandel who eventually won the Nobel Prize, tested the brain cells of sea slugs and found that with very little training of only forty impulses, motor neuron connections can be reduced from ninety percent to ten percent. So, Kandel wrote, "synapses can undergo large and *enduring* changes."

Well now. If forty delicate impulses can lead to abandonment of eighty percent of connections between neurons, imagine what the *eight-and-a-half* daily hours of
constant screen watching do to our neuron connections
that were once in frequent use with deep reading and
deep thought, that allowed people to concentrate, to
make "their own associations, draw their own inferences
and analogies, foster their own ideas"? What has the del-
uge of staccato bits of unconnected information done to
our "originality of thought and creativity of expression .
. . the hallmarks of the model mind . . . the center of art,
science and society"?

Maybe we should hurry up and tweet someone to find
out.

BUT THE BAD news gets worse. It seems that we have
two kinds of memory, short-term and long-term. Envision short term memory as a revolving door letting
things in and spewing them out. Long-term is more like
a vault, where memory is kept for years or even life. The
problem is that changing a short-term memory into a
long-term one is no simple task. One essential element
is repetition—"the neurons grow entirely new synaptic
terminals" hence causing an anatomical change. And
as Kandel states, "The growth and maintenance of new
synaptic terminals makes memory persist."

The formation of long-term memory, or what he calls

"complex memory," requires "system consolidation" or "conversations" between entirely different areas of the brain. This "memory consolidation" requires not only time—some scientists say hours, others days—but also attentiveness, "strong mental concentration," in other words "intense intellectual *or* emotional involvement."

Kandel now writes his most important conclusion, "For a memory to persist, the incoming information must be thoroughly and deeply processed. This is accomplished by attending to the information and associating it meaningfully and systematically with knowledge *already established* in memory."

The final element needed to create long-term memories is quiet time.

With the continuous and intense surfing of the web, distracted by hypertexts, streamers, pop-ups, and videos, our minds are constantly bombarded by stimuli; our memory is on overdrive. There is no down time, no reflection, no chance for the mind to even begin consolidating, or forming "schemas." And there is certainly no time for new neurons to be formed even if our poor brains could decide where to form them.

So this is where our Rhodes Scholar who has cast away books goes wrong when he believes that instead of slow and considered reading, he can go on the web and "absorb relevant information quickly." He may be surfing quickly, browsing quickly, even stopping to *look at* facts quickly but, for his long-term memory, for his *complex* memory he's *absorbing* little or, nothing at all.

ASIDE FROM ASSIMILATING little, the active parts of the brain develop, while those parts left unused, wilt and atrophy. So let us go to an extreme. Let us say one browses the web all day, sends abbreviated e-mails, tweets, and texts, then goes home and plays a few video games; then, to "relax," watches his obligatory five hours of TV. The only rest his mind gets, the only quiet time for complex memory to form, is while he's brushing his teeth.

The above, I fear, is much closer to the norm than to the exception. It is thus conceivable that one's complex memory, the seat of one's *self*, the source of thoughtful judgment and wisdom, is almost never engaged. Little by little, what small part had developed through the years, namely the complex part of our brain, shrivels. Of course, I suppose it could be slowly rebuilt, regenerated with use, but exactly when would this new, unaccustomed use occur? What would trigger it? And in a world made up of multiple screens and sound-bites, who would even bother triggering it at all?

ONE FINAL OBSERVATION. Carr cites the work and comments of Antonio Damasio, the Director of USC's Brain and Creativity Institute. Damasio and his colleagues have found in experiments that the higher, more noble human emotions such as compassion and empathy, are slow to form in a situation; it takes time to comprehend and feel the "Psychological and moral dimensions of a situation ... If things are happening too fast, you may not ever fully experience emotions about other people's psychological states."

Let us go back to the question I posed chapters ago; what happened to Wall Street? How could some of the world's brightest minds bring the world to the edge of financial chasm? How could they be so stupid? What were they thinking?

I believe the answer lies in neurons. First, the financiers of Wall Street were *not* stupid; they were brilliant. They were brilliant at browsing and surfing, at skimming information, at buying and selling at the blink of an eye, at reacting to blips on a screen, to two-word news flashes, to pop-ups and to flags. They were even superb at reducing the world to numbers where the only thing that counted, the only single goal was—at the end of the day—to have a larger number showing on the bottom of the screen. True reality, the rest of the world, countries, people, mothers, fathers, grandfathers and children, sad or laughing, suffering or happy, never entered what we can call, without malice, their "equation."

In other words, the working memories of our financiers were frantically and permanently "otherwise engaged." Meanwhile, their complex, long-term memories, their wisdom, empathy and compassion shriveled day by day.

Think of this new generation that grew up with remote controls, and video games, Web surfing and tweeting, constantly distracted, and often overloaded, when did it have time to form complex-memories? When did it have time to rest, think deeply, reflect? And when did it have time to feel compassion, sympathy, not to mention empathy?

Unfortunately a new study by the University of Michigan shockingly finds "almost never." Analyzing the personality tests of 13,737 college students over a 30 year period, between 1979 and 2009, the researchers found a 48 percent decrease in empathy and a 34 percent decrease in perspective-taking—considering someone else's point of view.

The authors of the study note that the biggest changes have occurred since the year 2000, with the inundation of callous reality TV shows, and the explosion of social networks and texting, which allow people to disengage from others at the click of a key. They blame these "physically distant online environments" for encouraging people to "lionize their own lives" and "functionally create a buffer between individuals, which makes it easier to ignore others' pain, or even at times, inflict pain upon others."

Mary Gordon, the founder and president of Roots of

Empathy, also cites a "poverty of time" in families. "You have to experience empathy to continue to develop it. If children don't have enough opportunity and parents don't have enough time to be with their children, it's really difficult."

As our lives accelerate, as our attention span is shredded, will there be any of us with a complex-memory left? Will any of us have that unique set of schemas, the brain's vital paths, whose infinite array of combined experiences—physical, intellectual and emotional—made each of us so miraculously unpredictable, volatile, spontaneous; unique? Without empathy and deep emotions, when we are only indistinguishable flickers of keys and gleaners of information, then how close do each of us come to being clones?

CHAPTER 15

Our Inner Depths

JUST AS THE ferocious pace and constant distraction of the Net atrophies our ability to "read deeply," so it robs us of that even more vital function we only touched on: to think deeply. I don't mean unraveling complex philosophical entanglements, far from it; I just mean looking at everyday problems and considering *all* their possible outcomes. Deep thinking has always been a prerequisite of human survival, today more than ever before, when very few men, in a very short time can bring us all to the brink of economic collapse, environmental disaster, or indeed annihilation. The ability—and, perhaps more importantly, the practice—of considering all aspects of a problem; of imagining the results of multiple solutions; and most crucially "perspective taking"—seeing the world from another's point of view—are all now at risk. Our modern mode of thinking is more and more limited to: yes or no, with us or against us, black or white.

The global crisis which this hurried, shallow thinking can lead to, is self-evident. What is less perceptible is that our shallow thinking combined with constant social networking may lead to a veritable human loss: the loss of deep emotions. How so?

I think you'll agree that our most profound and memorable emotional experiences occur under two very different conditions. One is when we are intensely involved with someone close to us, a lover or friend, face to face, *mano a mano,* heart to heart. The other is in solitude.

Face to face

Friends and lovers we deeply trust. Around them we are open, unguarded with our thoughts and emotions. This one-on-one is so important that most of us spend our lives searching for and then nurturing that special relationship in which we feel complete, in which we can enjoy life or face the world, or both.

Genuine friendship, the Swedish proverb says, "Doubles our joy and halves our sorrow." But genuine friendship also teaches us how to fit into the natural and human world, first by reinforcing our beliefs but, just as importantly, by challenging and questioning them. Thus, true friendship is not only a place where we feel free to open up or create, but it's also the perfect crucible for our ideas. But as Georgia O'Keefe said, true friendship takes time. It also takes a lot of patience, nurturing and forgiveness. And it takes being thoughtful when we're in a hurry; it takes caring enough to see beyond the meaning of words to their intentions; it takes feeling the helplessness of a friend's pain or struggle. And whereas these things are a vital part of life, most of our hurried network friendships furnish almost none.

Real friendship is measured in intensity and depth; its cornerstones are reliability and trust. A true friendship gives you many rights but just as many obligations. Electronic friendships demand little of us, and give not much in return.

There is no doubt that social networks are a convenient way to stay in touch, yet most often it's staying in touch with people to whom, until now, we couldn't be bothered to send even a postcard. By emphasizing the quantity of friends instead of their loyalty or caring, social networks reduce friendship to a commodity. Indeed electronic friendships seem to be mostly measured by numbers. And when friends are merely totaled up, *collected*, then friendship is no longer that unique, profound experience that brings out our very best, the most human in us. It's just collecting, and that's merely a hobby, like collecting baseball cards.

Of course you'll say what's wrong with collecting friends? And therein again lies a virtual friend's crime, for just as eating junk food leaves no room for the nutritious, and TV and video games leave no time for people, so virtual friends leave no time for real ones. Virtual friends only *rob us* of real life.

And apart from lacking depth and reliability, electronic friendships lack those magical moments when we find out we're indispensable to someone. Those moments happen so rarely even among true friends, fleeting moments when something is profoundly shared—a joke, a laugh, a squeeze of the hand, some news of pain or joy—that we often treasure them through life in deep memories, that make us feel good in the darkest night.

JUST HOW IMPORTANT do we deem the intensity of one-on-one face time? I'll cite one example.

My writing collaborator had been with her partner for five years. They'd considered and joked about marriage, but were both independent, even cynical New Yorkers, so they went on with life. Until one autumn day, they were heading back from a friend's wedding in New England, when, he drove to a quiet spot with a beautiful view of the fiery-colored hills. She was tired, just wanting to go home. He insisted they sit on a bench and look at the blazing colors down below. He recited a poem, which was not unusual for him, and then, completely unexpectedly, pulled a small, worn jewelry box from his pocket. From the box he took out his grandmother's slightly tarnished, and much-too-large, diamond ring.

Then he asked her to marry him. She laughed and cried simultaneously through the four-hour drive back home.

Basking in the thrill of it, she told no one. Not in e-mails or on Facebook, not even on the phone. She waited, biting her tongue, until she saw each of her friends face-to-face. "I wanted to tell them in person," she said. "I wanted to share their reaction, their surprise, their joy."

And even now, though months have passed, she will not put it on her Facebook page. She thinks that would somehow lessen its power, rob it of the magic.

Solitude

In solitude we can sink into ourselves, luxuriate in joy or suffering without bounds, and eat all the chocolate truffles we want. We can forget the passage of time and bask in the warmth of some ancient memory, reflect on the meaning of life or the color of our nail-polish, or let our fantasies, our hopes and dreads wash over us. Solitude allows us to be our own analysts, our own doctors, our personal trainers, advisers to our lives—or it can drive us crazy. Whatever the outcome, it allows us, at our own pace, to work out, then hopefully iron-out, our mental warps and kinks.

WE AMPLIFY THE richness of solitude when we experience it in nature. It seems to be the perfect setting for finding inner peace. Solitude in nature tends to let us find our place in the world; lets us feel a part of it; makes us belong. The immensity of nature, whether a starry night or the view from a mountain top, gives us a new perspective on life, washes away or minimizes our worries. How can we feel sad with all the beauty there to see? And how can we feel poor when all this beauty belongs to us?

It is fair to say that a good portion of man's great insights, whether scientific, philosophical or religious, were come upon in solitude. And almost all religions value the sanctity of solitary encounters with nature, from the Christian hermit in reclusion in a forest to a Buddhist monk in the depths of a still garden. As Emerson so wisely pointed out, "in the woods we return to reason and to faith."

I'm fortunate enough to live in the countryside. The views from the house are long, on clear days we can see the Isle of Elba, with a low winter sun even a glitter of the sea. There are vineyards and olive groves and woods around us but there is also the telephone, the computers and the doorbell. It might seem indulgent, but sometimes I need to get away.

There is a creek in a canyon as rocky and hidden as the hideaway of Saint Francis. By its side is a small field where the people from the five houses on our plateau hid their families and animals from the Germans during the war. It is a place of silence now where even the wind

doesn't come, where only the murmur of the creek wafts
through the still air. It is a good place to find solitude,
peace. The stillness tends to turn you so into yourself
that you might have thoughts you didn't really want,
about love, about loss, deep fears or sorrow. Yet after
every visit there, I come out feeling cleansed as if the
creek and the silence had purged me of all ills.

And in solitude I have time to gaze at the small wonders of the world, the first swelling pink bud on the
almond tree, finches pecking at shriveled, fallen olives,
a heron staring motionless at the pond, the billowing of
clouds, the ice-blue edges of the sky.

These might seem like trifles, and perhaps in and of
themselves they are, but noticing them, appreciating
them will lead to a lasting appreciation of the small
things in life, each of which can lead to a moment of
happiness or calm. And what is life if not some strung
together moments?

I have been lucky to have known deep solitude, from
singlehanded sailing among the Society Islands of Poly-
nesia, to climbing solo the rugged peaks of the Dolomites, to photographing for a book the dark, deserted
canals of Venice during long, desolate nights. The memories that remain of emotions felt then are some of the
most luminous of my life.

In those times, any "connectedness" to the outside
world would have lessened the depth of feelings.

And the more we stay "connected," the more being *not* connected seems like down-time, or like being left out. The beauty and richness of solitude becomes incomprehensible to us, and indeed interpreted as social rejection; a loneliness, that should be deleted as soon as possible.

The more our memorable emotional highs of both intimate companionship and solitude fall by the wayside, the first replaced by tepid virtual friendships, and the second by constant input, the more life becomes an existence without highlights. Our passions and emotions reduced to a hum, life becomes like mood music at the mall: no *grave* (slow and solemn) no *allegro* (fast and bright), no boisterous highs, no heart-rending lows; kind of there but barely noticeable.

CHAPTER 16

Talk to Me

OUR CLAIM TO fame as a species, and perhaps our apex of achievement—tap dancing aside—has been our abil ity to communicate with one another using words. The invention of expressive, thoughtful words raised us above the grunts of pigs, the howls of wolves, and—at least until recently—the twittering of birds. Without words we would most likely still be just another pack, herd, or flock struggling day to day merely to feed ourselves, and hunting and pecking so our friendly banker could not yank our hard earned nest out from under us. Without words we would still be inarticulate blobs whose major entertainment would be watching Alfa males butting heads on Monday nights, or eating fermented berries until we tripped in our three-inch heels and fell on the floor dead drunk.

Then we invented writing. With it, we gradually began to put deep and complex emotions into words, which until then only the most articulate and bravest (or drunkest) among us had the courage to do. It might be rash but justifiable to argue that the complexity of our emotions and the intricacy of our ideas ramified and grew as our written language bloomed.

Our innermost feelings we shared with those dear to us in cherished notes and letters which we assumed would be seen only by our intended recipient, and perhaps kept and treasured for a long time.

The fact that for millennia we wrote letters by hand, added much to the richness and depth of our experience. Since corrections were difficult and revisions time consuming, we tended to organize our thoughts in advance, most often with care, at times even with pride. And because a response was often weeks or months in coming, what we wrote stayed in our minds a while, as we worried about how what we wrote might be construed. Were they the best words? In the best order? How will she take them? What if she misunderstood?

And apart from the words themselves, there was the mark of the hand that formed them. The soft easy curves, or jagged, urgent lines, carried a message of their own, as unique and personal as the choice of words. Lest we forget the tearstains at the top, or kisses at the bottom, which placed into our hands a piece of the writer's heart.

When our communication accelerated to electronic

chatter, words became road kill. Emailing, tweeting and instant messaging add to the dilution of language. To be fair, many personal phrases had already lost their meaning. I'll never forget the first time a friend rushed toward me on the street, flashed a smile, blurted out, "How are you?" and without waiting for an answer, indeed without breaking stride, rushed by. From that day on, that phrase, for me, was dead. Its demise was assured without hope of resurrection, once it became fashionable for store clerks you had never met to inquire rhetorically, "And how are you today?"

More crucial phrases suffered the same fate. A numbing trend was introduced a few years ago when suddenly every subject from politics, to business, psychology and philosophy was discussed using sports terminology. Suddenly nothing was ever real again; wars, famine, human suffering were all reduced to "players," "game plan," "fourth down," "goal-line-stand," "squeeze play" and "grand slam." It was only a short step from that belittling of reality to dismissing blown apart men, women and children of wars as "collateral damage." Real descriptions, which elicited true emotions were deemed too hard to stomach (it might keep you from reaching for Cheetos in the news break) so we reduced human agony to a term that sounded like the title of a parlor game.

The next mania was the use of acronyms. This was most handy in Iraq where, because we called weapons of mass destruction WMDs, their non-existence didn't really matter, for their lack was no more troubling than forgetting mayo in your BLT.

And now we have new interjections: OMG and LOL.

Our emotional language is slowly atrophying. Our words, whether emailed, Facebooked, blogged or tweeted, seem most often thrown down in haste. While their spontaneity may be commendable, they reflect not only a lack of emotional involvement on our part, but also minimal concern for the feelings of the reader.

And when words are carelessly pitched, they quickly lose their power and, soon after, their meaning; they have no more impact than an artificial "How are you today?"

Some argue that words are superfluous anyway, that a lingering glance, a touch, a hand squeezed a moment too long, can express a closeness, a passion a thousand words can't. I couldn't agree more. But those moments of wordless face-to-face fervor are getting rare, because we simply no longer have the patience or the time. So we text.

AND WHETHER EMAILED or texted, we have a sense of unease that our messages aren't private. Perhaps because they can be instantly forwarded or twittered to the world, perhaps because they can be hacked into or looked at by anyone picking up our iPads or BlackBerrys, the privacy and security of old-fashioned letters are gone.

And with the loss of handwritten letters, meant for the eyes of that lover or friend, we have also lost one of life's great emotional rewards: Expectation. With postal mail there was a buildup of drama as we awaited a reply, speculated as to what it might contain, watched the road for the postman, our hearts sinking when nothing came, then finally pounding in our throats the day it did. Then we took that precious letter to a quiet place to savor words written for no one else but us.

I remember the first time a non-special message arrived from a dear friend. It was long before emails and texts. The message was on paper, but it was not hand-written or even original typewritten, but a photocopy. It was a Christmas letter that addressed me as "Dear _____," the blank filled with my name. I felt with that greeting our closeness was gone. Obviously the letter wasn't written to only me; it was also written to people I had never met. Its contents had nothing to do with the troubles, joys and fearful months of boatbuilding the friend and I had spent together; it was a newsy chat, no more personal than a notice in a local paper. It was long, full of facts—interesting, but it did nothing for my heart. Instead of feeling that we had reconnected, I felt only the loss of one barely remembered.

CHAPTER 17

Strangers in the Night
(and Day)

THE UNIVERSAL ADMAN'S image of human close-
ness is two lovers on a promontory, backs to us, entwined,
sun going down, golden light bursting, and mood music
effusing. What we don't see or hear are their cell phones
vibrating, their fingers twitching over text messages
and the cords of their MP3 players hanging from their
ears.

As if our social exile wasn't quite complete by dividing
us into marketable age groups, sticking us into isolating
houses, and isolating jobs, we are driven apart even more
by attention-demanding electronic gadgets. I'll give but
two short examples of how it all began.

We lived in Paris in 1982. Parisians love to talk—
their whole economy is based on it; bars, bistros, and
restaurants survive only because people get together for

an *espresso* or *un verre* or meal, but mostly for intense conversation: personal, philosophical and invariably probing. Hence most encounters between friends end up being memorable, exhaustive events.

A dear friend was driving me to a *soirée* and, as always, she talked about, what else: lovers, sex, lies, loss, and new lovers. We were having a good talk, open and honest; we were confidants, just she and I in that little Citroen, and all of Paris a backdrop. Then all of a sudden—for the first time in my life—a brand new device, her car-phone rang. She answered and chatted. She might as well have pushed me from the moving car. Our intimacy, solemnity, the deep trust of the moment was no more. A distant had come between us; suddenly there was someone else with us in the car.

I hope you don't think me melodramatic but the shock of that moment is still with me today.

Of course now our cell phones ring any place, any hour, whether we're dining, or driving, in bed or on the moon—and we almost feel like social outcasts if it doesn't. So we say we are now used to our social moments being interrupted, we say it's all part of life, we adapt, we go on. But do we? The next time you're having a special moment with a lover or a friend and his or her phone rings, close your eyes. Don't listen to their conversation but listen to yourself—how does that make you feel. Happy? Joyful? Or ignored? Even betrayed? Just see if your heart sinks, and your spirit sags as the preciousness of that moment is lost.

THE SECOND ELECTRONIC blow to social intimacy came a year later. We were living in New York in an old loft in Soho at a time when Soho was still nothing but boarded-up storefronts and garment sweatshops. Candace and I shared the loft with her best friend at art school, Giovanna. New York went through hard times then, the Lower Eastside was a near war-zone, the subway stops were reeking dungeons, many a subway car without lights or with doors that wouldn't shut, the only reliable thing inside and out was graffiti.

But there were also truly good times, outrageous, spontaneous art, an explosion of impromptu galleries and eateries all over the East Village, late nights in bars, great blues music, deafening sounds in discos, wide open rowdy parties, and vivacious street life at all hours among the gutted buildings.

My shock came one Saturday afternoon. My head was throbbing with a hangover and my jaw sore from an altercation with a drunken yuppie who had insulted a painter friend. Giovanna decided we needed a quiet getaway on a boat that circumnavigated Manhattan. It was a beautiful spring day and the sights were fine. We laughed a lot, which made my sore jaw sorer, but it was fun traveling with two rowdy, pretty women. During a lull in conversation, Giovanna pulled out her newly acquired pride and joy, a Walkman. She put on her headphones and turned it on. To us she might as well have jumped over the side. She was gone. She no longer talked to us or heard us, or saw what we saw, or felt what we felt. It was as if she had slammed a door in our faces.

Twenty years later, these invisible doors are slamming in our faces dozens of times a day. When the cell phone rings, we tell ourselves that we're tough and stoic, we can withstand these small rejections, but it's these miniscule letdowns which strung end to end make up our lives and form us.

Whether we verbalize it or not—they affect us, harden us; bit by bit, they close us. And as they close us from each other, we drift apart, our conversations become more shallow, our laughter more mechanical, our sympathy more feigned.

If we can become thus distanced from our friends, just imagine how distant we are with perfect strangers. Not only do we no longer know or love our neighbor but, quite frankly my dear, we don't give a damn. And if *we* don't give a damn, why would the banker, who is about to foreclose on our house? Why would he even blink before he kicked us into the street? The banker sees his position clearly in the world: he's all alone doing his job, looking out for Number One.

Many would object, saying that these small isolations, the weakening of social bonds, have no great effect on the world, that more important things affect our daily lives. Think again. Take what happened to politics for instance. As a vast majority of Americans agreed in the 2010 midterm elections, Congress and Senate were doing a dismal job. The Democrats and Republicans had developed so much animosity that dialogue was almost impossible: everyone ranted, no one listened. This intransigent partisanship was not a condition that developed overnight; it snuck up over the years, like global warming, like the rabid financial system, like our dying neighborhoods.

Retiring Senator Dodd, who joined the senate thirty-six years ago, lamented that over the past two decades there has been a "stripping of the socialization, which is always what made this place function."

He remembers the late hours in the members' dining room, where senators mingled, where he sat enthralled listening to the old bulls. "As a new member, you just sat there and absorbed it as they would rib each other and sometimes have a heated debate about a subject," he says. "It was as good an education as you could get about the place."

Today, "there's no one in that room."

WHILE SOME GADGETS drive us apart, others keep us from ever coming together. The best example is that true marvel, the GPS. You just tell the little lady in the box where you want to go and she will get you there; all you have to do is turn on your ignition and turn off your mind.

The reassuring female voice tells you to slow here, turn there; it's like directing an old cart horse but with electronic reins.

I admit there is a relaxing brainlessness to the process, and most often the thing will get you safely where you were heading, aside from a few notable exceptions like the lady in Canada who, obeying her GPS, drove miles into a bog; and another in England, who drove into a river. On a daily basis, more than half the people coming to our house from Florence or Siena using GPS get lost; the last family so much so, that at one point their GPS fell into a coma.

For most of us, the GPS can turn travel into a disorienting void. A friend drove from London to his house in Tuscany using a GPS and said at journey's end that half the time he had no clue where he was, and, upon arrival, felt as if he hadn't been anywhere at all.

Others complain of going numb, with no thought and no reasoning; just sitting, waiting for the next command. One friend did notice that his GPS cut down marital fights; instead of shouting at his wife, he now shouts at the lady in the box. And she, instead of responding by crumpling up the map, just murmurs sweetly, "Turn left at the next right."

A GPS, aside from shutting down your brain, keeping

it from attentive observation, from doing basic arithmetic and simple problem solving, also tends to set your trip
in stone. Once you key in your destination, you tend not
to improvise, to veer off and take some small road on a
whim, or head off toward some intriguing hillside town
on an isolated coast.

But apart from that, there is a social sacrifice: the
human contact you miss out on when you're undecided
or lost. I have traveled worldwide on author tours or
just for the pure love of it, and have learned to rely on a
simple electronic/voice device: I push a button, the car
window goes down, and I yell out, "Where am I?"

It works every time—invariably someone, eventually,
responds.

Some very fond memories are from encounters of the
lost kind. I'll never forget the dapper young Italian who
stepped from his car into the pouring rain to explain the
complex streets of the historic center of Ravenna to me,
only to end up laughing at his own confusing instructions, jumping back in his car and shouting, "Follow me."

In Guatemala, Candace and I were taken under wing
by three brothers and, not only given directions, but also
ushered into their mother's house for lunch, then taken
on a guided tour around a magnificent lake. Or the time
in Sicily, when undecided between two roads, one along
the coast and one inland, both marked green, meaning
scenic, we stopped in a small town to ask local advice.

Candace got out of the car and asked a local lady. The lady considered, looked at the map and gave longwinded directions. A gentleman passing by stopped and waved his arms. "That road there?" he exclaimed, "I wouldn't send my in-laws on that mule-trail." The crowd grew. Soon there were six of them explaining, cajoling, countering, "Yes, but this has the view . . . but that one has the lake . . . but on this you can stop at Luigi's for *pranzo*."

Last Sunday we drove out to the sea to visit some Etruscan ruins near the town of Follonica. We arrived just before lunch and looked for the place a friend had suggested for excellent seafood. We got lost so we stopped at a small car repair place. Not only was the old mechanic happy to help, but also began advising on the best dishes on the menu. Upon arrival, we were greeted by a sign marked "Closed for holidays." Back to the garage. The mechanic began to scratch his head then his eyes lit up. "Va bene," he chimed. "I have it. Great food and romance," and he described a place on piling jutting into the sea. He yelled after us, "And tell them to treat you right because Mimo sent you!"

The view was stunning, the owner friendly and gossipy, just the way we like it. The *tagliatelle di mare* and the *pinci* with clams in pesto sauce were to die for, the mixed seafood grill fresh as the sea, the bottle of *Vernaccia* was superb and the bill came discounted nearly 20 percent.

I'll never forget Mimo's smiling face, or the setting, or the meal. Not something the lady in the black box could have arranged.

These are admittedly small, fleeting events. None of the people became lifelong friends, or lovers, or sent us birthday greetings, but the memory of those meetings—brief human encounters, that come when you need them most, when you're the most lost, forlorn or hungry—are encounters that restore your faith in human warmth, in simple generosity, in unremunerated caring.

THEN THERE'S THE pride thing. Candace and I have sailed many coasts and open waters, starting decades ago when all we had was a sextant and a compass. Nowadays, especially offshore, or off an unknown coastline, Candace, who navigates, wouldn't be without her beloved GPS. I, on the other hand, never learned how to use it. Twice I had to sail big boats without her, solo.

Once was on a borrowed boat, sailing from the island of Raiatea to Bora Bora—about twenty miles. A storm had come through the previous night and big seas still ran in the morning, so from the trough of swells, all I saw was sky. The wind stayed high throughout the day and the sloop ran with all her might. From the top of the swells, I could spot the mountains of Bora Bora, but I couldn't for the life of me see the only entrance to its lagoon: a narrow cut in the reef now covered by breaking waves. The trip, with a lot of gybing to avoid running wing and wing, took me seven hours. I made three runs at the reef to find the opening, twice I had to turn just boat-lengths from the coral, but, when I finally made it, I felt as proud as if had just circled the globe alone.

In a life as regimented and "safe" as most of ours tend to be; where we are seldom challenged, or called upon to think afresh, invent or improvise, I'll happily take some chances, even risks, get lost, make mistakes, try again, just so that at day's end I can have that incomparable sensation of having made it on my own; of having used all my senses, and been completely "alive."

THEN THERE ARE the games and apps our children appear to be attached to night and day, whether in cars, in their rooms, or at the dinner table. Exactly what posi-tive contribution parents think they are making when buying them this stuff, I have no clue.

Parents rave about how new apps keep their children from getting bored on drives. Hello? What ever happened to gazing out the window, looking at the scenery? And even if the scenery isn't always majestic, even if it's a ghetto or industrial slum, is it not a good idea that they see it and think about it, so when they grow up and run the world they can remember how awful those places tend to be?

Even at the dinner table, game apps and iPads seem to be the norm. I saw a Russian family in Verona, sporting all the right jeans and longed-for shopping bags, sitting down in a good restaurant with their two children of around ten years old. They had barely pulled in their chairs when one child whipped out his iPad and the two of them started watching a movie. Not only did they not interact with their parents or each other, or barely notice the food they were shoveling into their faces, but the volume of the movie disturbed adjoining tables. Did the parents mull it over before Christmas to come up with the best package for teaching their children social isolation, culinary ignorance, absolute disregard of others, and how to be the most obnoxious children in the room?

Is it any wonder that some of our children grow up self-centered, uncaring, bored, and socially inept? How could they be anything else when parents put such anti-social weapons in their hands?

So what's the solution? Turn the gadget off. Or, better still, don't buy it in the first place. Brett Arends, a financial columnist for *The Wall Street Journal*, a paper about as conservative and technology-admiring as there is, wrote recently "I dumped my iPod Touch . . . The scarcest resource in life isn't money, land, fresh water or gold. For singles under 25, the scarcest resource is sex, and for the rest of us it's time. And the biggest waste of time I've ever discovered—after games—is the Web. Nothing comes close. It's a total black hole."

CHAPTER 18

Let Us Play

"Too little playtime may seem to rank far down on the
list of society's worries, but the scientists, psychologists,
educators and others who are part of the play movement say that most of the social and intellectual skills
one needs to succeed in life and work are first developed
through childhood play."

— *THE NEW YORK TIMES,* JAN 6, 2011

TO APPRECIATE JUST how important playing is we
need only ask the ultimate experts: our kids. Any kid will
tell you that playing is not only the most exhilarating
but also the most joyously memorable part of life.

While our society now loosely defines play as anything
that's not schoolwork or homework, scientific experts
define it as, "a game or activity initiated and directed
by children." Accordingly this leaves out not only most

regimented video games and TV watching, where the only thing a child directs is his frozen gaze, but also most organized activities and sports.

Real play is something kids do independently and by themselves, without adults, their orders or instructions. Most modern toys, however, especially educational ones, also "direct," leaving kids little to imagine or create. Real play then is that with the fewest props. Has any part of your life been as breathlessly exciting as the games of tag or hide-and-seek you played?

Whether it's mucking about in a sandbox, building a raft from sticks, or a seesaw from a log and a board, or a fort under the table with a sheet and cushions, one thing that will stay with you for life, is the firing up, and constant use, of your imagination.

And when real play is in a group, you learn not only how to keep your imagination aglow, but also how to function well together, in a miniature society. Apart from thinking creatively you discover how to compromise and how to blend your talents in with those of others: to work as a team. And you learn how to take care of the smaller ones or weaker ones; you learn how to nurture, how to help.

A true miracle of real group play is that it brings out the best in every child. It may sound cliché, but in a group we get a chance to discover who we are. I don't mean this in some existential sense, but simply that in a group any given child will quickly find out not only his weak points but also his, perhaps heretofore undiscovered, strengths. While his delusions about being a great athlete might be shattered, he might instead become cherished, like Eddie Emanoff, as the funniest biped alive. Or, he could turn out to be a great mediator of people, resolve their differences, calm their fears; as we discovered in our gang with Dave Dowsett, his quiet good nature and reasonableness made him a perfect leader.

In short, real group play, unorganized, unsupervised, uninterrupted by adults, will give any child the freedom and time to grow. It might not teach instantly measurable skills, or raise SAT scores, but he will bloom in other departments: in being an open-minded, understanding, in-love-with-life human.

IN THIS AGE of solitary TV watching, video games, play dates and soccer moms, it's pretty plain that real play, whether group or solitary, has been left behind.

Michael Rich, the director of the Center on Media and Child Health at Children's Hospital in Boston, worries about how much play has been replaced by TV, computers, and technology. "We're denying them a childhood," he says "How many kids are going to remember that great Angry Bird game? But if they climb a tree with their friend, they'll remember that. That's what we're trading off."

I remember with absolute clarity going into the woods

on a wintry afternoon, armed with a hatchet, a small spade, matches, a sausage and some bread. After starting a fire, I tried to imagine where the ancient fortress must have been; its entrance and watchtower; where the jewels of queens and kingly crowns lay buried. Then digging, dizzy with excitement, and finding bits of clay pots, convinced that the gold was just a few more shovelfuls below. When I got tired, I skewered the sausage, roasted it slowly over the coals, and toasted the bread. The smell of both mixed with the damp forest fragrance. Then I wrapped the sausage in the warm bread blanket and ate with hungry bites.

This happened on the hill behind our house, just before dark today. The excitement and the joy I felt, over what most people would call absolutely nothing, is something I learned long ago as a child. Without knowing at an early age how to find my own fun, create my own play, imagine my own ancient cities and hidden gold, I would probably not have even bothered going into our woods.

Arguably the most useful intellectual faculty we can cultivate is imagination. With true play, based on a few toys, we have to invent characters, situations, whole worlds. All that will serve us well in adult life when we have to conceive whole scenarios and potential outcomes, most often based on a few clues, personality traits or details.

And, quite opposed to electronic gadgets, which teach us that any impulsive nervous reaction brings instant response, real play teaches us patience, not only with ourselves and the world around us, but when playing with others, we learn about their rhythms; their sense of urgency or lack thereof; we learn that there exist various senses of time.

It is perhaps ironic, but certainly telling, that Shigeru Miyamoto, the most respected inventor of video games like Super Mario, grew up without TV or video games in a small village west of Kyoto. What fired up his imagination, his sense of mystery and wonder were his solitary walks in the wooded hills, in bogs, creeks and dark, twisting caves.

He says he felt sad for modern urban children who were robbed of the same intense, real life experiences he had, so he tried to create the games for them as a substitute. But in a virtual world, no matter how clever or convincing, there is no mystery or discovery that comes close to the intensity of real life.

I remember the terror I felt when I was six, and one summer afternoon my friends fearlessly crossed a creek, but I stayed behind because I had heard it had leeches that attach themselves to you and suck your blood. I stood there alone, imagining what horrors would befall me if I crossed and slipped and fell. No video game, not even zombies and chainsaws, can be as intensely horrifying as that.

SO WHAT WILL happen if our kids don't live real lives? As we saw from a neuro-scientific perspective, vital paths of our brains, like paths in fields or forests, are formed by frequent use. What if we lead mostly virtual lives where everything is provided to us, where every experience is just a flick of a key away, where the risks aren't real, nor is the fear, nor the rush, nor the joy? What if we grew up without mystery or wonder? What if we grew up never having to really imagine? Would then the vital path to our imagination simply be overgrown from lack of use, or would it—more sadly—never have formed at all?

Real play teaches more than just imagination. It builds unshakable *self-confidence*. In sharp contrast with the rights and wrongs of directed play, in real play there are few wrongs. Take something like a sandcastle. Most sandcastles do not come with directions; you just dig and pile. Shape, size, and design are up to you. However you build—providing it stays up—you will have succeeded.

Having created something from nothing, and the exhilarating *possibility* of that, will stay with you for life. It will also teach you that you can *control* your world, not just the flickering lights on a screen, but the brawny physical world where you can build hills and dig canals, and, for a few breathless moments, even hold back the tide.

Once you learn real play, you'll never know boredom. Being able to use what's at hand, whether it's something to observe like nature, architecture or people, or something to do like kicking a cigarette box on the subway platform while waiting for the F train, will—besides raising some eyebrows—keep you forever and constantly engaged, involved: entertained.

Apart from the simple fun of it, real play serves another purpose. Just as eating junk food keeps you from eating real food, and virtual games keep you from playing real ones, so, *in reverse*, real play will so fill your life that there'll be no room for the fake; and no need to game, text, or tweet every minute. It will save you from depending on electronic drugs.

Then there is the physicality of it. Much alarm has been sounded lately about our children being overweight and obese. Less talked about is their immobility. There is a vast difference between the athletic muscle structure, heart-and-lung capacity and physical coordination of a two hundred-and-fifty pound defensive lineman, and of an equally heavy but barely mobile, video-gaming dumpling.

How this sedentary society came about is absolutely amazing, given that our species' genetic programming makes us only slightly less physically jittery than gazelles. Just watch a child once he learns to walk. He doesn't: he runs. In fact most kids have but two speeds: sleep and overdrive. Just how TV and computers have managed to immobilize us as effectively as a body cast, shows you the horrendous power of both beasts.

I swear on a stack of bibles that my childhood gang didn't have an ounce of body fat *combined*—except for

Eddy Emanoff whose mom and dad were Russian and stuffed him with borscht, piroghis, sausages and sour-cream morning, noon and night. Our parents stuffed us too, but we were all as thin as any Dorothea Lange kid from the depression, not because we didn't eat well but because we *moved*. Nonstop and mostly at full-bore. No one lifted weights, or went to kiddy-gym or had personal trainers, we just played. Ran, jumped, skated, played scrub baseball, touch football, rode bikes and stopped only to tie our shoelace.

So if you love your child, do something simple and highly cost-effective: deprive him. Of everything. Everything except real home-cooked food and lots of love and hugs. The rest he'll find himself, all you have to do is dress him and then shove him out the door. The real world with real kids, just like him, is waiting.

But Play Where?

Recent, mounting studies and statistics suggest that the culture of play, worldwide, is vanishing. In addition to the electronic menace, a major problem with the world being eighty-percent urban, is lack of space to play. Back in Budapest we could not care less, we had a perfectly good soccer game in front of our apartment on the cobble-stones, with horseshit for goalposts and the ball made of rags, although we'd have to stop the rare time a truck or a horse-cart waddled by. With today's traffic, play-space must actually be provided, yet according to a recent Center for Disease Control survey, eighty percent of children do not live within walking distance—that's a half-mile i.e. a ten minute walk—of a playground or a park. Why?

A society aglitter with towering financial palaces, one that has countless miles of freeway and shopping malls and parking lots whose combined surface area would obliterate New Zealand, can't manage to give its children an empty lot to play in? Hello? Is there really *anybody* home? If we can have a million laws that guarantee freedom and the pursuit of happiness, can we not have one guaranteeing every neighborhood a patch of empty ground?

I WITNESSED THE apex of our insanity a couple of years back in, of all places, Vancouver. When I lived there long ago, it was a laid-back town with the second largest hippie culture after San Francisco. No more. It got rich.

We were visiting relatives in North Vancouver, a hilly suburb below a snow-clad mountain, and, as usual, I got restless indoors and decided to go for a walk. After a few blocks, I came across a playground. It had both a manicured baseball diamond and a soccer field, the grass was well cut, the fences in good shape. I thought what a great country; until I saw the sign.

It had struck me as kind of odd that in the middle

of summer, the middle of the day, there wasn't a kid in sight. My old gang would have been swarming over the fields with joy. Except for the sign. It said in large black letters with each word underlined, "Unauthorized playing strictly forbidden. Minimum fine $200." I nearly lost my mind. I don't often fly into rages—ok, sometimes I do—but that!

I went back to the house, got a soccer ball, and ran around on that field and kicked it against that shiny backstop as unauthorizedly as I could.

Just look at New York's Central Park on any given Sunday. Mayhem. There are acres of fields without borders or fences, just some scattered backstops, but witness thousands of exuberant "unauthorized" humans of all ages, shapes and sizes, playing every kind of game man has invented; yelling, laughing, running completely wild.

Exuberantly alive.

BACK IN BUDAPEST, even on the coldest winter days, my Grandmother would order me to bundle up and go out into the sunlight and fresh air to play. When I objected, wanting to stay inside, she would tuck in my scarf, plunk the wool cap onto my head and unceremoniously march me out the door, uttering her favorite slogan: "Sunlight and fresh air. You are not a fungus." Remember that, and a whole new life will follow.

CHAPTER 19

Teach Your Children Well

"America is losing sight of its children. In decisions
made every day we are placing them at the very
bottom of our agenda with grave consequences
for the future of the nation."

—A *CARNEGIE FOUNDATION* REPORT

STRANGE HOW ONE can see the world's flaws clearly
yet miss the same glaring defects in one's own life. I was
writing about the Carnegie report years ago, lamenting
how a society could be so shortsighted, so neglectful, and
all the while I was letting my own son slip to the bottom
of my own agenda.

Buster was in his first years of school in Tuscany, and
we had just found an ancient ruin to restore near Siena.
There were plans to be made, permits to get, the future

to be dreamed of. For two years, while my priorities were the precise curvature for arches, the ideal beams for the roof, and where to find the nicest antique tiles, Buster and his needs, including his schoolwork, were mostly ignored. He hung on, but it wasn't easy.

He was always a kid in motion. Living in the country he was used to having room to roam, so being confined to a desk, especially with all those tempting kids around to play with, broke down his willpower every now and then.

By grade four, he was a demon. His teachers loved his warmth, sense of humor, and passion but not the fact that he was uncontrollable. When we saw his grades slip, we took him out of school and for a year taught him at home.

It was heaven. We didn't have to get up at dawn to catch the school bus; we could have a week's holiday nearly every month and drive to Paris, or Granada, or take a ferry to Greece.

But it was also hell. Neither Candace nor I were teachers—I had only substituted part time during my last year of college—and while that didn't deter us, doing his homework in Italian sure did. Buster would translate the assignment into English, then we struggled through the work in three languages (we argued and swore in Hungarian), at the end of which he translated it back into Italian.

I'm not a patient man. I often rattled his chair to stir him. It clattered on the tiles so downstairs Candace knew our progress by whether it was a three or four-chair rattle that day.

A retired teacher taught Buster science and Italian, I did history and geography, and Candace did math, French and art in a blend. To be credited for the year Buster had to write an exam in each subject plus do a two-hour oral before thirteen judges. The next day one of the judges stopped us on the street and congratulated us not only on his knowledge but his alertness, confidence and sociability.

The next year back at school he was the best in class.

I did not write this just to put you to sleep, nor to glorify Buster, and certainly not to glorify us. Since our abilities as teachers were minimal, and our patience even less, and *he* certainly was no dedicated student, the good results suggest that he did so unexpectedly well because he had been propelled from the "bottom of our agenda" to the top. He loved it. And so did we. That year, we became much closer as a family.

MOST STUDIES NOTE that society outside the school, our home life, neighborhood life, our whole cultural emphasis, has infinitely more bearing on how our children will do scholastically than the school itself. And the recommendations of the Carnegie report, which found "35 percent of students started school unprepared to learn," are equally broad-based, ranging from job-sharing and more flexible hours for parents, to less mindless children's television programs, more parks, kids' tours for a broad range of stimulation, closed streets for safe play, and more adult contact and involvement.

In short—if you'll allow me a simplification—kids who sense that they and their schooling are important to those around them, will do well. Otherwise, if no one cares, why would they?

To prove this point on a worldwide scale, I offer the following two reports.

How to Make a Trillion

The Organization for Economic Co-operation and Development (OECD) has as its stated mission "to promote policies that will improve the economic and social well-being of people around the world." Among other things, every three years it compares how different countries' school systems are readying their young people for modern life. Its 2009 report which measures student performance in reading, science and mathematics among 15 year olds in 34 countries, shows the top three countries—Finland, South Korea and Singapore—so far ahead that the bottom 10 percent of Finnish students are level with the median pupil from the US. Specifically the US has slipped to 14th rank for reading skills, 17th for science, and 25th for math.

What is the importance of all this? With nationwide cuts to manage runaway state budgets—Texas is considering eliminating 100,000 jobs in education—the conclusion of the OECD report might just stop every politician in his tracks. The OECD has worked out a formula showing how a country's scholastic performance in fact *determines* its current GDP. The OECD's conclusion is not only shocking but should instantly mobilize a rethinking of the education system. Its calculations show: "Bringing the United States up to the average performance of Finland, the best-performing education system among OECD countries, could result in gains in the order of *103 trillion dollars.*"

Yes, you read it right: $103 trillion.

Now that's serious money, enough to cover the federal government's current deficit for about a hundred years. In all fairness, the payoff would not be instant, but spread over the lifetime of the new generation, i.e. 75 years. Still, that means that raising scholastic levels could produce an extra 1.3 trillion dollars every year; about a third of the 2010 US budget. Just think of the possibilities all that money could buy. The boys on Wall Street would never have to worry, they could drive us over the brink once a year, and the country—as in 2008—could smilingly bail them out.

Another report, by McKinsey, found that the achievement gap between the US and top performing nations imposes "the economic equivalent of a permanent recession on the US."

An interesting comment about the shortsightedness of our actions was made by columnist Bob Herbert of *The New York Times*. "What a country. We'll do whatever it takes to make sure the bankers keep living the high life and swilling that Champagne while at the same time we're taking books out of the hands of schoolchildren trying to get an education."

In other words the question again is really that of agendas. The OECD states that in order for America to start the climb toward the top, it has to "make the choices needed to show that (it) values education *more* than other areas of national interest." In other words: forget the curvature of the arches, shapes of beams and color of the tiles and focus the agenda first and foremost on the kids.

The potential $100 trillion windfall aside, the importance of the OECD study is *not* which country ranks highest, but what lessons and new directions can be learned from the countries at the top. I don't mean just lessons that would only improve education or even the GDP, I mean cultural lessons that we want to apply to the enhancement of society as a whole.

The Huffington Post's Justin Snider interviewed Dr. Pasi Sahlberg, Director General of the Centre for International Mobility and Cooperation in Finland's Ministry of Education and Culture. He asked the obvious question "How did Finland do it?"

Sahlberg began by challenging old assumptions. First he felt that increasing the time spent studying is futile, instead he thought, "The important thing is ensuring school is a place where students can discover who they are and what they can do." (And all this time I thought it was a place to rattle chairs.)

Next he acknowledged that while most of the creative educational ideas came from the US, the big difference was in how Finland applied them. The Finns, he said, consider education as "nation building." Education has to be run and directed not by business administrators but by former teachers.

He also shrugged off the new craze of measuring a teacher's performance. "Finns don't believe you can reliably measure the essence of learning."

Sahlberg concluded with something that we should apply from the cradle. "You know, one big difference in thinking about education, and the whole discourse, is that in the United States it's based on a belief in competition. In my country, we believe in cooperation and sharing. *Cooperation is a core starting point for growth.*"

I can't help but be reminded of Roseto, where cooperation in the community was placed far above competition; and that "particular egalitarian ethos of the town, that discouraged the wealthy from flaunting their success and helped the unsuccessful obscure their failures."

While we're downgrading flaunting and upgrading cooperation, we might stop and reflect on a statistic from

NEA Research. "The current ratio of the average salary of Fortune 500 CEO to that of an American public school teacher: 200 to 1." I have one question: what kind of society will we end up with when someone who makes car-wax or nail polish earns *200 times more* than the person who shapes our children's minds?

THERE IS NO magic bullet for instantly improving an education system, but one thing that needs to change immediately is people's thinking. A massive fifty-page paper on what needs to be done came from McKinsey & Company, management consultants and advisers to the world's leading businesses, governments, and institutions. I'll try to condense it here to two pages. After exhaustively studying the worlds' most successful school systems—those of Finland, Singapore and South Korea—they came up with a shockingly simple conclusion: "The quality of an education system cannot exceed the quality of its teachers."

And they elaborated. "A number of the world's top-performing school systems have made great teaching their 'north star.' They have strategic and systematic approaches to attract, develop, retain, and ensure the efficacy of the most talented educators, and they make it a *priority* to attract and retain top graduates to a career in teaching."

The aim of the paper was, "to describe how these

high-performing school systems have accomplished this, and to share the results of original market research on what it would take to attract and retain top students to teaching in the United States."

So how did the top countries do it?

Well, apart from making cooperation "the core starting point," all three countries, use a most rigorous and highly selective system to "recruit, develop and retain only 'top third plus' students into the field of education." 'Top third' means choosing 100 percent of their teacher corps from the top third of the academic cohort (in the US it's only 23 percent). Once chosen, applicants undergo further screening. That's the plus. All are screened for qualities found to be predictors of teaching success: perseverance, ability to motivate others, passion for children, emotional intelligence and communications skills. As a result, in Finland only about "one in ten applicants is accepted to become a teacher." In the US there is no screening.

The amount of national prestige and cultural respect this gives teachers is reflected in a comment by a Finland education expert, "People know that if you've been trained as a teacher you must really be something special." Partly owing to this prestige, "teaching is the most popular career choice and the most admired profession among top students, *outpolling* law and science."

In short they make sure they have *great* teachers, and

that great teachers serve students of all socio-economic backgrounds.

Nowhere is the adage, "You get what you pay for," truer than in this instance. Out of 29 countries surveyed for teacher compensation, the US came in 23rd, only slightly worse than where it stood in scholastic achievement on the OECD tests. In sharp contrast, to make teaching an attractive career, most top countries not only *pay* all of a student's tuition plus a stipend, but also make sure that starting salaries and progressive salaries match other careers in the market place. The average starting salary in New York City in 2007 for teachers was $43,000; for lawyers *nearly four times more*: $160,000.

When you combine a good living—the report calculates that a South Korean teacher's purchasing power is 250 percent that of a US counterpart—with good vacations, social prestige, and the life-long job security Korean teachers are guaranteed, it's little wonder that, as with the Finns, teaching is the most popular career choice among young Koreans.

When you add to the above, that the best countries provide their teachers with a pleasing, stimulating, and safe work environment, it is easy to see why the very best students these countries have end up teaching the next generation.

The McKinsey report concludes, "Ignoring these nations' examples would be to stake America's future on the questionable idea that the U.S., alone among nations, can prepare its children to thrive in a global economy while relying on lower-achieving graduates to teach them."

A closing comment in the report merits attention: "In stark contrast to the three top performing countries, the US does not have a national strategy for the teaching profession."

Strange, when you give it some thought. There is a national strategy, training and machinery—not to mention an astronomic budget—for fighting endless wars, yet there isn't a national policy for how to make the nation's kids smart enough to avoid them.

What now?

Lewis Mumford might have been right on the money when he said, "We have to begin all over again at the very beginning, with the infant in its crib. That is where education starts."

We might begin by liberating our children from the Kiddie Ghetto, where the Kiddie Industrial Complex dictates their whole lives. If you think I'm exaggerating just look at Kiddie Food, Kiddie Toys, Kiddie Gyms and Kiddie Shows.

Some claim these give children their own world, and that's true. But it's a tiny, artificial, desiccated world, where nothing is ever wrong and everyone always smiles. It is a world cut off from grown-up reality, cut off from the variety of adults with a variety of problems, and most often a variety of ways of solving them. Not only do kids miss out on constant contact and affection, but also on real life: listening, reasoning, arguing. The real adult world might at times be confusing, unpleasant, and even wrought with pain, but just as often it's filled with laughter and love, concern and caring. And, whatever else it will be, it will be rich in complexity and emotion, and will give children not only an understanding and appreciation of their own species, but just as important, a sense of belonging in it.

Among this fragile, joyous lot they might find some real heroes, not the superheroes and wizards their Kiddie world abounds in, but vulnerable, ever-changing, puzzling, messy humans whom you can hate like hell one minute and love the next, who might just give them some ideas of what they might like, and not like, to grow up to be. And they might then grow up with an insightful, deeper view of life, and might learn how to create a more humane world.

Hunger for Learning

Over the last generation, many who still show an interest in learning, do so not seeking wisdom but to merely to pass tests, to get a diploma, get that steady job. Even in the most enjoyable of subjects, English literature, which to me was story-telling on school time, teachers complain that students don't bother to immerse themselves in the work, but become increasingly dependent on "explanations" of pieces of literature, containing outlines and comments.

In other words, our children are not learning to think. Like the Rhodes Scholar philosophy major in chapter 14, they are simply perfecting the act of transferring information from here to there without putting themselves in between. They are not learning to form opinions or gain experience, feel passions or even make interpretations; they rely on answers coming from outside. It is no wonder then that they grow up to accept mind-numbing careers, and elect half-witted politicians, because they're used to doing as they are told; they have learned that answers lie in someone else's condensed view of life.

Just one last anecdote.

During my last year of university when I substitute taught high school students to get by, I did everything from Spanish (my total knowledge was "Eso es un robo," which I learned from *Butch Cassidy* and means "This is a holdup") to senior girls' Phys. Ed., where I barely knew where to look. And I taught some English.

One day I got a class of ninth graders who had almost finished reading *The Lord of the Flies*. I looked at the questions the *real* teacher had left behind, one was, "Who is the Lord of the Flies?" And she wrote the answer down. I asked the class. Hands flew up. I picked the scholarly-looking kid and of course his answer was "right." I said so. The class went silent. I was about to move on to the next question when a street-wise-looking kid thrust his hand in the air. He gave another answer. For once in my life I had the wisdom to not contradict. Then I asked him to explain. He did, with rough syntax but clear and bright reasoning. I was floored. More hands shot up and the class began to buzz. Hands waved, words flew and faces got excited. They explained, they argued. Almost every one of those little guys had an answer, a *different* answer, his or her *own* answer, from his or her *own* mind, *own* heart, *own* interpretation, *own* life. To hell with official interpretations, to hell with William Golding. *They* had read the book, *they* had thought it through, *they* had felt it through, and *they knew!* And by God, they were right and no one was going to tell them different. I had seldom felt so alive. And I felt honored to be with them. That was in 1969.

No one in the world knows how to live life to the fullest as a child does, inventing a million silly, inconvenient, laughable, and magical ways to be human.

When J. D. Salinger first saw a photograph of the little boy adopted by Lillian Ross, he wrote, "He's roaring with laughter. Oh, if only he can hold on to it."

Whatever it takes to keep that spark alive, whatever creativity, whatever effort on our part, it should be done. No. It *must* be done.

CHAPTER 20

All You Need Is Love

"In a society as highly organized as Western culture, a person depends upon many other people and upon conditions in general for his security. This means, of course, that a person's security may often be threatened or lost through no fault of his own. For that reason, security takes on a special importance in people's lives—more so in many cases than other human motives—and it is responsible for much personal unhappiness."

—DR. CLIFFORD T. MORGAN
AND RICHARD A. KING, *Introduction to Psychology*

The Insecurity Industry

Not long ago our security—or at least our sense of it— was all but assured: we belonged to a village or a neighborhood, and we were sought out for our friendship or loyalty or good humor. And we were respected not only for qualities like wisdom or honesty, but for visible skills and contributions like building houses or teaching school, baking bread or curing the sick. Yet, vital as it is, we seem to have at some point lost our sense of security, for modern urban life rarely offers such reassuring niches—and even more rarely now that both craftsmen and the life-long steady job have all but vanished.

The jobs we do have are often so fragmentary as to be barely describable, thus appear to have little or no merit. And we often work anonymously so that even if our contribution is appreciated, it is done in distant silence. Lastly, few of us produce anything tangible, so it's difficult to look at our work with pride, and say to ourselves, hey, that was a job well done.

Meanwhile, society, instead of compensating for our lost security by creating a nurturing and humane environment, actually fuels our new *insecurity* by hyper-inflating the cultural importance of such superficial inventions as Success, Fame, and Perfect Physical Beauty.

LET'S START WITH the last one since it's the media favorite. As if modern women didn't already feel enough pressure to have a successful career and be a sex goddess, wife, mom, and homemaker, now magazines, TV and the Web, inundate them with images of stunningly bone-structured, "perfectly" shaped women, meaning sky-scraper limbs and wispy waists. The Social Issues Research Center estimates that today's girls, "see more images of outstandingly beautiful women in *one day* than our mothers saw throughout their entire adolescence." The problem is that the ideal size combined with the ideal face, is achievable by less than 1 percent of the female population. If you throw in ideal age, which seems to be between seventeen and twenty, then the percentage goes down to . . . forget it.

As a consequence, a recent study found that 92 percent of teenage girls would like to change the way they look. Nearly 75 percent feel "depressed and ashamed" after only three minutes of flipping through a fashion magazine, and most frightening of all, 70 percent of girls ages 15 to 17 avoid normal daily activities such as attending school, going to the doctor, or even giving their opinion "due to feeling badly about their looks." So badly that 25 percent consider plastic surgery.

How we got to this depressed state has little to do with our kids' appearance and more to do with our hectic lives, which leave little time for close contact with our children. Studies have found that people suffering from extreme body-image disturbance report a lack of holding and hugging in childhood, so it can be theorized that the lack of physical contact has at least some effect on the less extreme cases.

But the most astute conclusion as to why most women have a wretched self-image, was unflinchingly summed up by The Media Awareness Center. "By presenting an ideal difficult to achieve and maintain, the cosmetic, fashion and diet-product industries are assured of growth and profits. Women who are insecure about their bodies are more likely to buy beauty products, new clothes, and diet aids. It is estimated that the diet industry alone is worth anywhere between $40 to $100 billion a year selling temporary weight loss . . . Over three-quarters of the covers of women's magazines include at least one message about how to change a woman's bodily appearance—by diet, exercise or cosmetic surgery."

In another study, 90 percent of the women surveyed agreed that happiness is the primary element making a woman beautiful, and that they themselves feel most beautiful when they are happy and fulfilled. The sad irony is that the number of women who *felt* "beautiful" was only 2 percent.

THE QUESTION AGAIN remains, *what* are we missing out on while we're busy doing the wrong thing, in this case trying to buy socially-correct beauty? For as we chase these elusive media ideals, meaningful self–improvement which could greatly enhance our true beauty passes us by.

There is a celebrated old saying that "beauty is in the eye of the beholder." Wrong. Take it from someone who profoundly loves women: true beauty is in the eye of the *beholden.* Some natural calamities aside, most women have the potential to be breathtakingly beautiful, but it has to be a genuine deep beauty: fervor for life, a love of humor, honesty, curiosity, caring, all things that show irrepressibly in the eyes. Ok, let's broaden that and include a heartfelt smile, which, just as much as the eyes, is shaped by what's inside. I can't tell you how many times I've seen a fine-boned woman whom society would call gorgeous, only to be turned off by the shallowness in her eyes or the insincerity of her smile.

The problem is that making ourselves *truly* more appealing—wiser, more thoughtful, full-of-life, curious, witty, caring, loving—is a time-consuming, subtle and often lengthy task, so we tend to obey the urging of the media instead. We shop.

Any visit to a mall will demonstrate that the Insecurity Industry depends on us buying stuff we never wanted, stuff no human being could possibly ever *need*.

Many will say buying a few things can't be all that harmful, it passes the time or makes you feel better when you're down. True, but therein lies the danger. The good feeling you get from shopping is the most shallow and temporary of emotions, and not only does it rob you of the time you could really be improving, but it makes you sweep aside your fundamental problems. And problems swept aside pile up until one day you will trip over the mound.

A classic example is the behavior of a friend's daughter.

The parents divorced when the child was eight. She interpreted the divorce as rejection by her father. On her visits with him, when she felt panicked or depressed, instead of talking out the problem, he gave her a couple of hundred dollars to go shopping and feel better. He meant well. But she spiraled slowly down into severe anxiety, and alternated between feverish shopping sprees and huddling in a corner. The only notable improvement was that she huddled in new clothes.

As our life trickles away searching for things to buy, we forget all the things that are ours for free: the seashore, the meadows, the mountains, the woods—where we can find some peace, a sense of belonging, a sense of self: where we can beam with the inner beauty of serenity.

Success

When the media isn't flooding us with high cheekbones, it tries to impress us with very successful—measured in dollars—men.

A few years ago, maybe five, there was a front-page article in a *New York Times* Magazine. It featured one of America's most famous and wildly successful entrepreneurs. I don't recall his name, just that he was the CEO of Walt Disney or Sony Records or the universe. The article went on for many pages about the deals he had pulled off, blockbusters he had produced, things he owned, billions he had amassed. At one point, the writer asked him about his friends and relationships. The man fell silent. Then he said—he was in his forties—that he'd been so busy that he hadn't had the time.

I'm no anthropological biologist but I bet you have to look pretty far down the evolutionary ladder to find a species that glorifies one who lives without mates or friends.

I realize that to condemn success may at first sound like treason, but we must acknowledge that it is mostly a western, media-driven society obsession. Again Drs. Morgan and King point out that, "We are taught that in the land of opportunity everyone can succeed . . . if only he works hard at it. And success is highly prized. The picture is very different in other cultures."

We witnessed a remarkable demonstration of this in the recent rebellion in Egypt. During the eighteen days of uprising, while tens of thousands risked their lives, not a single person jumped to the forefront to stand out, to be famous, to take over and claim success in leading the revolt. It was a group success, just like the Finnish education system; it came about because of general cooperation.

I bring it up mostly because it seems that we have made a tragic substitution, confusing financial success with lasting happiness. A *New Yorker* piece by Elizabeth Kolbert pointed out how completely unrelated these two really are. She cited a 1978 study of lottery winners who had pocketed between fifty thousand and a million dollars. While they all agreed that winning was a highly positive experience, they considered themselves no happier than a control group of Illinoisans who had won nothing at all. And even more surprising, the control group of non-winners reported getting more pleasure from their daily lives.

In his book, *The Social Animal*, David Brooks nicely settles the money/happiness question. "Research over the past thirty years makes it clear that what the inner mind really wants is connection . . . Joining a group that meets just once a month produces the same increase in happiness as doubling your income." I'll go even farther and say that our newly found obsession with financial success has in fact caused *un*happiness and has made all of us just as insecure as the obsession with surface beauty and ideal body shape made teenage girls.

The World Health Organization and Harvard Medical School jointly conducted a study based on more than 60,000 face-to-face interviews worldwide, and found that the United States has the highest rate of depression among 14 countries. This unhealthy emotional state was confirmed by a recent survey of the American College Counseling Association who found that 44 percent in counseling have severe psychological disorders; that's up from 16 percent in 2000. This is almost a three-fold jump in just one decade—the common disorders being depression, anxiety, suicidal thoughts, alcohol abuse, attention disorders, eating disorders and self-injury.

In a broader 2009 survey, The American College Health Association found 46 percent of college students felt "things were hopeless" at least once in the previous 12 months; 31 percent had been so depressed that it was difficult for them to function; 15 percent suffer from clinical depression; and 10 percent have seriously considered suicide.

So why are so many of us in such mental misery?

Since the study of teenage girls tends to point to a low self-image caused by social pressures i.e. media barrage, I think we can safely assume that the collective unhappiness of the rest of us is caused by social pressures and the same media, only instead of pushing the "beautiful," this time it's the "rich and famous," or children of the rich and famous, or dogs of the children of the . . .

I'm at a loss as to the motivation for this media barrage unless it's an unspoken conspiracy to keep us focused relentlessly on money in order to assure that this goods-obsessed culture remains forever in place. I mean, what would be wrong with a TV series called the "The Poor, and Unknown"? Or, to combine it with self-improvement, one titled "The Secret to Instant Poverty."

And if the media wasn't enough to drive us over the edge, we have helicopter parents and tiger parents urging us on with the most mind-boggling slogans like, "Grow up to be somebody."

Is this a joke? Am I not somebody now? Should I grow up and be somebody else? Who? Elmer Fudd? Mary Magdalene? Attila the Hun?

Then there is, "make something of yourself." Like what? A cup and saucer? Skirt and sweater? An oak dining-room set? Give me a clue! . . . If slogans like these won't propel us down the road to schizophrenia, what will?

I mean really, what the hell is wrong with us the way we are? Why should we become anything or achieve anything? We are already miraculous creatures; we walk, talk, tell jokes, some of us even yodel. We even like each other if given half a chance. Can't we just stop achieving for a while? Sleep in 'til ten, then hoe our veggie-garden or tidy up the house, then slouch down to the beach to check the surf, or go down to the creek and do a little fishing? Who needs the rest? Titles, career, power? As Mrs. Rooney cried out in a Beckett play long ago, "Christ, what a planet!"

Success at your fingertips

In order to save our sanity we have to redefine success. How can we look at monetary success with pride when the personal accumulation of wealth, measured in many millions of dollars, is led by investment bankers whose work has mostly been confirmed to be "socially worthless"? Can we be socially worthless and proud at the same time?

I agree that a decent level of income is comforting. I have had the good fortune of having my books sell, yet the money they have brought gave me only a moderate *feeling* of success. What counted more were reactions from readers, like the couple who took turns reading *Shipshape*, aloud in bed and going to sleep laughing; or the doctor, whose family discussed *A Reasonable Life* for weeks at the dinner table; or the Polish family who spent a day looking for our house, just to thank us for the joy a *A Vineyard in Tuscany* had brought them, and then shyly handed us a jar of their home-made jam. In those moments, I felt appreciated—I had managed to give someone a bit of happiness. In those moments, I was bursting with a feeling of success.

IN OUR SMALL town of Montalcino, Carlo, the butcher, has found great success—he works happily in his shop knowing that he is cherished for his excellent sausages and mouth-watering *prosciutto*. Giovanna, our baker, now seventy-two years old, is revered for her breads and cakes; our doctor Talenti for his genuine concern and instantly curative joviality, and our cabinet-maker, our black-smith, mechanic, post-mistress, and of course Giancarlo who helps everyone with everything, are all greatly admired and valued for doing their very best and adding to the well-being and happiness of us all.

Moments of true success used to fill our lives: we made things, cooked things, fixed things when they broke, and shared the joy of accomplishment with family and friends. They were all tiny achievements, but they formed social bonds, giving us a sense of worth and pride. We shared a lot of small social functions: cleaning house, sewing clothes, working the garden, cutting each other's hair, washing dishes, fixing the car, putting up a shed—those gave us something to do together, to talk about together, even bitch about together, and common things to bitch about form one hell of a tie.

But, little by little, we lost these daily functions, and with them the daily bonds. And with each loss, we lost the spark of self-esteem that came with having done something with our own hands, and our wit. They were tiny sparks, true, but tiny sparks can kindle a big flame. And, what makes these losses even sadder, is that those sparks of pride often had to do with the fulfillment of our basic needs: we maintained, with our own hands, our family, our home, our neighborhood; the foundations of our lives. And this left us with the secure sense that if the world went awry, if problems befell us, we could set things right—that we could always, if need be, fall back on ourselves.

I don't think this is sheer conjecture. A whole slew of programs such as Outward Bound, which teaches survival in the wilderness, are designed to build up self-esteem, by making the individual self-reliant, teaching him to look after his own basic needs. Just as our self-confidence can be built up by small experiences, so it can be lost by small deprivations.

Once we lose these anchors, we begin to have doubts. Is it any wonder then that we feel depressed, self-doubting, insecure? Is it any wonder we're not sure who we are? How important and to whom? And is it any wonder that we'd like to be someone else—richer or more beautiful—just in case that someone else has a better hold on life? And is it any wonder that, if we can't be heroes to our family, friends and children, we try so hard to be heroes somewhere else? The only question is, "Who will then remain to be heroes to them?"

The strength of our social bonds is continually ebbing. Sure you work your heart out at some distant, unseen place, even accumulate wealth, but to your children those are abstract things, they leave no memories in their hearts, not like the birdhouse that they helped you make, or the doll you sewed together, or the story that you told on some dark and stormy night.

REAL SUCCESS, OR more accurately, the feeling of success—for it is only that, a feeling—is much more personal than the number of zeros in a bank account. So it might be best for each of us to reflect on *when* we have felt successful, were filled with meaningful pride, and simply strive to create more similar moments. In short, we should all have our own personal definition of success.

I HAVE SPENT a few days reflecting with as much honesty as I could on the things in my life that have made me truly, unforgettably proud. There were readers reactions to the books, a few physical achievements like the solo sailings I mentioned, or climbing tough peaks in the Dolomites alone, but those were solitary joys, where I succeeded only in overcoming my own fears.

My most cherished moments of success are more

humble. The first was in my houseboat forty years ago, when, for our third date, I managed, with no experience, to cook a five-course Japanese meal for Candace. And not have it kill her.

The second was decades later. When Buster was nine, he was crazy about knights. He loved their castles, their horses, their righteousness, their swords. I couldn't provide the first three so I attempted the last one for Christmas. Secretly, at night, I carved a couple of wooden swords with nifty cross-pieces to protect the hands in battle, and I made some oval shields out of thin plywood with grips and leather straps. Sneaking out to the shed late one night to paint them, I forgot all about our centuries-old stone-lined ditch below the path. I did a four-foot fall onto a sharp edge which opened up my leg. I set a world record of consecutive *porca miserias*, but closed the gash with some butterfly sutures and went on with the painting. For years the thud of swords on shields filled the air in our courtyard, as Buster and his friends battled each other for land, for honor, for hours.

There wasn't much value in those swords and shields—I could have bought a shiny plastic set for a pittance—but there was something else that came with them that money couldn't buy, something neither of us ever spoke about in these fourteen years, but neither of us has forgotten. It is still there. I can see it in his eyes.

A Letter from Debbie Apple
who is committed to leading a reasonable life

From the time my children were born, I wanted them to know true freedom. Over the past few years, we have found that freedom comes with a price, and we have paid dearly.

My first line in the sand against the mighty foe of commercialism was removing the television from our home. I bought a pile of board games and traded my son the games for the television. How could any 5-year-old resist those colorful boxes? Sneaky, I know, but it worked. Years later, after my daughter was born, we had guests over for dinner who brought four young children along. Several times I overheard "Don't you have a TV in here?" At the end of the evening, waving at the red tail lights in the driveway, my daughter grabbed my hand and said "Mom, don't we have a TV?" "No Honey, we don't."

She tightened her grip, looked at me with trust and said "OK."

I knew I would homeschool and follow the method of a British Minister of Education who believed in teaching the "whole child." What could children learn about life, others and themselves without being in the woods or a pasture? My children learned math by counting eggs and figuring out how many gallon jugs they would need if the cow's milk filled the 80lb milk can. Latin set a good foundation and Logic was a preemptive strike against the world's advertising. Language came from great classics read by the fireplace. Biology was taught in the garden and in the century-old barn that had seen more birth and death than I could imagine.

In 2008, we went to work on a certified organic farm, taking with us our chickens, cows and sheep. My 17-year-old son milked and cared for the animals while I looked for a market for our produce, and my 11-year-old daughter Rhayna kept us all straight and helped to keep the kitchen going.

Money was king at this farm (I managed to increase sales by over $30,000) but there was no time for friends and family. People fell to last place and the stress loaded onto our shoulders was more than we could handle—we craved peace. So, with two children, 50 chickens, 30 cows and 15 sheep, we found ourselves farm-less. We placed the animals on the unused land of friends.

Amazingly, we lacked for nothing. We had the best food, warm clothes, great books and a loving family. I remember a wise priest told me that my family was reality; everything else was illusion. I had two great children who loved me and loved each other. We worked and played together. What else could we need?

Unfortunately, banks do not lend on such sentimental assets and I couldn't buy a farm. Family came through and we moved in with my brother and sister-in-law. My son drives 40 minutes every morning to milk the cows and care for the animals, I try to keep the customers happy and assure them that we are keeping up our end of the deal by providing healthy, delicious food for their tables, and Rhayna continues to keep our heads on straight.

Throughout this time my mind sometimes triumphed over my heart. I would ask myself, "What are you doing? You can't keep this up forever. Be reasonable. Just get a job at the mall and put the kids into school. Let go of this foolish dream." But my heart cried out to hold on and keep trying.

Today, I see that I have planted the seed of conviviality in my children's hearts and even tough times cannot kill that. I found a small property and hopefully will be able to get financing within a month or so. Several young people in the neighborhood plan to open a shop downtown with a used bookstore, a pub, a local food forager (me) and bakery in one building. They have big plans for us and we are thrilled. They too have the seeds of conviviality in their hearts, seeds that only needed a bit of watering.

The only inheritance I will leave my children will be a piece of ground, animals we loved and served and that served us. If I can teach them to listen to their hearts above all other voices, I will have given them a beautiful life and I'm good with that.

You can check out Debbie Apple's Windy Acres Farm Shoppe, which offers natural, gourmet meats, cheese and other products, at www.WindyAcresFarmShop.com.

A Reasonable Garden

By Eliot Coleman and Barbara Damrosch

FOR MOST PEOPLE, growing their own food is just a dream. We believe it is a possibility. There are ways to integrate food-growing into our lives that are simple, non-technological, time-efficient, and above all, pleasurable. What we need is a new approach, a reasonable garden.

We all lost out when food production became a complex industry rather than a simple process. The soul of the household was removed from our lives and put into the hands of "experts." Why? When a simple natural process becomes complicated, whether it is giving birth, growing food, or burying the dead, it is always because some industry is trying to sell us products or services for its own benefit—but not necessarily for ours. Somehow we get caught up in these arrangements to the point where we assume there is no way out.

Much has been said in recent years about the risks to our health posed by the way our food is grown. From the moment a seed is planted to the moment the fruit enters our bodies, our food comes in contact with so many substances having known or suspected ill effects that we tend to give all of it a glance of mistrust. "Where has this cucumber been and what has been done to it?"

But most of the reasons for making food production a daily activity are positive ones. Participating in the profession of food from the garden to the kitchen to the table is an important part of the human experience. It involves us with the flavors and textures of foods so that we select the ones that give us the most nutritional value. Our own hand-dug potatoes or newly harvested peas are irresistible. Tasteless ones brought home in a plastic bag leave our palates unfulfilled, and we turn to sugary unwholesome fare by way of compensation.

If homegrown food is clearly better, why is store-bought food still the norm? Why not recover the simple joys of providing our own? When an obviously superior practice doesn't catch on it is usually because people perceive it to be more complicated and more onerous than the present one. Often a simple refinement of the idea is necessary to move from the contagious enthusiasm of a few passionate devotees to a practical reality for everyone. We believe that there are three mistaken assumptions that inhibit people from full participation in home food production. First, soil fertility is assumed to result only from very hard work or expensive soil amendments. Second, home gardening is assumed to be productive only in the summer. And third, food storage is assumed to require complicated equipment such as pressure canners and large, energy-consuming freezers.

A return to home food production requires more than a change of habits. It requires a rethinking of gardening methods. During the sixties and seventies there was a movement back to home gardening, but the way it was conceived kept the movement from achieving lasting success. People soon tired of the idea. Raised beds, double-dug halfway to China, seemed liked punishment. Extending the growing season failed because the methods used were more technological than biological. Elaborate solar greenhouses were complicated solutions that required endless tinkering and close attention. If you chose to can and freeze you faced long days and nights getting ready for winter before the garden labor was even finished. It was a puritanical philosophy of life that spoke of dedication, not celebration.

Because it seemed to involve so much hard work and

a great deal of land, home food production came to be regarded as an all-or-nothing proposition. It went along with chucking the whole system, returning to the farm, living outside the national economy, and making everything you needed at home. While there is much to be said for doing just that, it was not something many people embraced for long because it was so much more difficult than the norm. For behavior to change, the new idea must offer more reward than effort, and it must possess an elementary elegance in both conception and practice. An elegance, to quote Saint Exupery, which "had not been invented but simply discovered, had in the beginning been hidden by nature and in the end been found."

The elementary elegance lies in understanding gardening as a process, not as a goal. Growing food can be a comfortable, manageable part of your life, just as cooking is—something done a little at a time, as needed, not all at once in a series of overwhelming chores. Instead of the usual sequence—"putting in the garden," "bringing in the harvest," and "putting up food"—wouldn't it be better to have a garden that is "in" all the time, and a harvest that goes on all year, whenever fresh food is needed for a meal?

This sounds like something that would only be possible in a frost-free climate, or with a heated greenhouse, neither of which is available to the average person. But in fact it is easy to do without moving to the tropics or spending a lot of money. We eat fresh food out of our Maine garden every day of the year without a heated greenhouse, in a climate where the frost-free season lasts only three and a half months and winter temperatures can drop to minus 20F. How? By appreciating the unique abilities of various crops to do their best in their respective seasons; by growing them in a logically planned succession; and by respecting and working with the natural world. There are four components of the system: compost, cold frames, cool-season vegetables, and a root cellar.

Compost is the principal input that keeps a garden producing bounteously. You make compost in your backyard by layering organic materials to encourage air and moisture to permeate them. This allows the natural populations of bacteria, fungi, earthworms, and other creatures to create the dark, crumbly humus that bespeaks soil fertility. Since the ingredients for your compost heap are either kitchen and garden wastes—carrot tops, outer cabbage leaves, apple cores, eggshells—or plants that grow in your backyard—weeds, old grass, leaves, and stems—this wonderful product is both home produced and free. For extra compost ingredients you can easily replant lawn areas to high-yielding forage crops such as alfalfa and mow them periodically.

John Updike, in a poem about compost, noted that "all process is reprocessing"—a nice metaphor for this conception of the home garden as a cyclical process rather than a linear, goal-oriented chore. Compost keeps your garden going the same way the natural world keeps itself powered—by recycling organic matter. That's why it is so simple and successful. You spread compost on the surface of the soil and mix it in shallowly with a cultivator. No digging required. Plants grown in a soil amended with compost are not stressed for nutrients and are consequently healthier and more resistant to pests. Once you try using compost you will never want to be without it. Good compost takes a year to mature. The trick is to simply start the process and keep it going. "Making compost" is not a job; it is the remains of one season becoming the fuel for the next.

A *cold frame* is a low box covered with glass that sits on the soil. The sides of the box can be boards, longs, straw bales or concrete blocks. The glass covers on top are usually recycled storm windows. The size is any dimension that the available materials will cover. For taller crops, you make taller frames. The simple cold frame, which has been around in one form or another for centuries, is the home for your winter garden.

The protection of a cold frame tempers the winter climate. It takes the harsh edge off the extremes of the cold, the wet, and especially the wind. That slight moderation allows a wide range of cool-weather crops to be harvestable through the winter in all parts of the United States.

In far northern climates where the winters are severe, in order to harvest the full range of crops even during the coldest parts of mid-winter you may want to place some of your frames inside another layer of protection, such as a simple, unheated, lean-to glass greenhouse. The key is to provide enough protection to prevent the soil in the frames from more than superficial freezing. Each layer of protection is like moving the garden a zone and a half to the south.

Cool-season vegetables are the cold-weather equivalents of the conventional summer garden vegetables. Some 20 crops—both familiar ones such as spinach, leeks, kale, chard, carrots, broccoli, scallions, parsley and Brussels sprouts, and the less familiar like mache, claytonia, arugula, mizuna, dandelion, kohlrabi, chicory, cress, sorrel, escarole, endive and radicchio—thrive in the cold of winter with a little protection. These are hardy plants and are not harmed by the freezing on cold nights. During the day even weak sunshine will raise the cold frame temperature above freezing so you can harvest fresh foods for both salads and main courses. Cool-season vegetables supply you with six months of fresh food with almost no care, no pests, and no weeds.

Planting a little at a time makes the process of the garden continuous. After the various summer crops are harvested, winter crops are sown in succession. Most of their growing is done by late fall and, with roots in the soil, they remain fresh all winter. Many of these cool-season vegetables have become fashionable of late and appear on upscale restaurant menus. But in Europe, thanks to slightly more temperate winters, they have been traditional fare for centuries. They are not thought of as a substitute for summer foods but as a full palette of delicious ingredients in their own right.

The *root cellar* is a hole in the ground in which you can store root crops over the winter when they can no longer remain in the garden. Whether as substantial as the concrete cellars of colder climates or as modest as the buried barrels used where winters are less hard, root cellars take advantage of the natural coolness, dampness, and darkness of the earth. Cool and damp and dark are the ideal storage conditions for potatoes, carrots, beets, rutabagas, cabbage, celeriac and parsley root. Onions and squash prefer cool and dry conditions and can be stored in the attic or an unheated room. Drying is the best storage method for a winter-long supply of tomatoes.

A root cellar is an extension of nature's own system, since it contains crops that are designed to be stored underground. It needs to be sufficiently below ground so the contents won't freeze, but beyond that it operates almost automatically. As the weather cools down in the fall the earth cools, and so does the cellar. The high-moisture conditions required for optimum storage are supplied naturally under the ground. The darkness prevents sprouting in storage and keeps potatoes from greening. The crops in our root cellar keep dependably into June every year. By the time the earth and the cellar become warm in early summer everything is fresh from the garden once again.

When many people think of "extending the growing season, they think of prolonging summer crops. Such a goal can only lead in the direction of high-tech, high-energy systems. In this garden we are only "extending the harvest season" for those crops that don't mind cold. For every season there is a vegetable—corn, tomatoes, eggplant, and beans in the summer; spinach and peas in spring and fall; mache and chicory in winter. Preparing meals in harmony with the climate is a delight. Don't we get excited when, in a foreign country, we encounter an item on a restaurant menu that has just come into season locally, and is being offered fresh, cooked in a special regional way? The cuisines of the world were developed around seasons and regions. Our own lowest-common-denominator food system, based on nationwide, year-round sameness, leads to cooking that is boring and predictable. Eating seasonally keeps us connected with the natural world. We associate young dandelion greens with fragrant spring mornings, fiery chili with peppers turning scarlet in the sun, apple crisp with the bracing bite of autumn, hardy leeks with a robust soup simmering on the stove when you come in from a snowy walk. Just as it's easier to write a sonnet than free verse, it's easier to cook well with seasonal limitations. They are a spur to creativity.

But doesn't gardening year-round mean a lot of work? Actually, it is less work than trying to do it all in the summer. The trick is to garden little and often. Think of your garden as a patchwork quilt of different crops. You plant seeds in one small patch today and another next week. There is never a disaster when a planting fails, because there is always next week's planting, or next season's. Even thinning a row of greens becomes part of the ongoing process of gardening and eating: by consuming each week's thinnings, you put food on the table at the same time you are giving next month's dinner more room to grow. And winter is still a resting time for the gardener: the crops in your frames were planted in late summer and fall, and sit there all winter—fresh, flavorful, and ready to be harvested. Seasonal successions also mean you can grow a large variety of crops in a much smaller space than that occupied by the traditional summer garden that grows everything at once. Thus they're a perfect solution for the town or suburban gardener with the use of a tiny yard or community plot. Even in climates with the shortest seasons, a garden 30 feet square is smaller than the singles area on one side of a tennis court. The chart at the end of this appendix will give you some idea of the sequence of availability of different vegetables in a four-season garden.

If you have more space and time you may want to try raising livestock as well. A couple of backyard ducks are a much better egg source than chickens. They lay more, do well on homegrown food and simple housing, and they don't hide their eggs. They also don't scratch up the garden soil, and will eagerly patrol the yard looking for slugs. A backyard milk goat or small cow will provide fresh dairy products. Enough, in fact, that you may choose to share the produce and the care of the animal with a neighbor. But for the average homeowner with a regular job, raising animals is often too much of a commitment, and the answer lies in seeking out local farmers who produce animal products in a way that is humane for the animals and healthy for the consumer.

Fruits are also a home garden product, and definitely worth the effort. Small fruit trees or berry bushes can be planted as a windbreak on the north and west sides of the garden. A bed of strawberries can be included in the garden, with a new bed set out from healthy runners every year. Apples, over most of the country, are the easiest tree fruit to grown, and they store well in the root cellar. Grapes, raspberries, blackberries, and high-bush blueberries are the most dependable small fruit. Blueberries can be dried like grapes to make a "blueberry raisin," which lends a heavenly flavor to winter dishes.

Don't try to remake the whole world all at once in your backyard. Just start growing some food for your table that makes it central to your everyday life. Once you begin to enjoy the food, the process will achieve a flow of its own (Eliot's book, *The Four Season Harvest*, gives a detailed program for how to do it). Too often gardening is like the great summer vacation trip that has to make up for 50 weeks in the city. Make gardening ordinary, daily, a nourishing interaction with the natural world around you.

Organic Pest and Disease Control

Organic gardening means less work, not more. That applies especially to dealing with insect and disease problems. The aim of organic gardening is to understand, nurture, and enhance the systems of the natural world in order to produce food for human consumption. Pests have a positive role to play in those natural systems. Thus, spending long hours picking off bugs is no more of an answer than using pesticides. The same goes for garlic, spray, red pepper, herbal concoctions, or rotenone. All techniques that aim to forcibly remove insects, whether using chemical or organic methods, are counterproductive. They are all palliatives. The word palliative, from the Latin *pallium*, a cloak, defines any method that treats the symptom of a problem without curing it. From a common sense point of view the gardener who avoids toxic chemicals is to be praised. However, from the point of view of biological systems, the gardener who uses natural insecticides is no wiser than his chemical counterpart—different ingredients but the same mistake.

Insects and disease are not the problem. They are the symptom of plant stress. Their presence is a visible exterior indication that all is not well with the plant. No one would be so simple as to think that a child's chicken pox could be cured by scraping off the spots—the visible, exterior symptoms. Similarly, removing insects from a plant does not cure the problem or eliminate the cause. All that insect removal accomplishes is to pretend the problem doesn't exist.

The goal in organic gardening is to eliminate the cause of insects and disease rather than just treat the symptoms. When you begin to think in those terms a whole new world opens up. The plant bothered by pests need no longer be a cause for dismay. The plant can now be looked upon as your co-worker. It is communicating with you. It is saying that growing conditions are not conducive to its physiological well-being and that if the plants are to be healthier next year the growing conditions must be improved.

The idea of learning from your plants that something is amiss is nothing new. Any textbook on mineral deficiency in plants will contain pictures of the symptoms exhibited by plants in response to various deficiencies in the soil. A common example that many home gardeners have probably noted is the yellowing of corn leaves when insufficient nitrogen is available. The attack of insects and disease is just as certain an indication of unbalanced health as yellowed leaves. The remedy is the same: improve the growing conditions. To accomplish that goal you must determine what conditions are lacking for optimum plant vitality in your garden and then attempt to achieve them.

Take your lawn, for example. Say you have a lawn that is growing a crop of grab grass, plantain, and other weeds but few of the finer grasses that you would prefer. There are two courses of action. For one you could purchase all the heavily advertised nostrums, herbicides, fertilizers, and stimulants to try and suppress the competition and allow the finer grasses to struggle ahead. Conversely, you could study the optimum growing conditions for the grasses and then by adding compost, rock powders, peat moss, manure, aerating, draining, irrigating, letting in more sun, or whatever seemed indicated, you could create conditions under which the finer grasses will outcompete the competition. The advantage is that whereas the nostrums have to be resorted to frequently the growing condition improvements are more permanent. If you doubt this approach, look closely at wild vegetation. Certain groups and types of plants grow successfully in one area but not another because the conditions favor them. You want to create conditions in your garden that favor vegetables.

How do you determine the optimum conditions for the plants you wish to grow? A little detective work is in order. Closely observe the plants, the insects, the diseases, and every aspect of the garden. Are all plants affected equally or are those at one end of the row or in the rows along one edge not showing symptoms? What is the difference in the soil in those areas? Is that where you limed or didn't lime because you ran out? Did you compost that area with compost from a different heap? What was different about that heap? Is the good section of the garden where all the maple leaves blew in? Or where the corner of the old barn foundation was? Is it the new disease-resistant variety that is doing so well? Do you always grow the same crop in the same place every year?

If you can find no specific clues to follow, try a general approach to plant habitat improvement for next year. A crop rotation will always help. You might grow deep-rooting green fertilizers, add different types of organic matter such as seaweed to your compost heap, and supply adequate quantities of rock powders for minerals. Think about aerating the soil with a garden fork to break up soil compaction or removing the branch of tree to let in more sunlight. Evaluate all the possibilities and then organize your responses.

Palliatives are a deceptive trap. Removing the symptoms may seem to improve the situation, but it is only a cosmetic improvement. Since it doesn't solve the problem you have to do it over and over again. Whereas momentary reliance on palliative treatments is understandable, they should never form the basis of your gardening practices. Creating optimum growing conditions is the one constructive approach in a dependable long-range philosophy of gardening.

•

BARBARA DAMROSCH is the author of *The Garden Primer* and was a regular contributor to PBS's *The Victory Garden*.

ELIOT COLEMAN is the author of *The New Organic Grower* and *The Four Season Harvest*. He has been the Executive Director of the International Federation of Organic Agriculture Movements and an advisor to the U.S. Department of Agriculture.

SEASONAL AVAILABILITY OF FRESH GARDEN VEGETABLES

FRESH ▣   STORED ■

VEGETABLE	SPRING Mar 21-Jun 21	SUMMER Jun 21-Sep 21	FALL Sep 21-Dec 21	WINTER Dec 21-Mar 21
Artichoke		FRESH	FRESH	
Arugula	FRESH			
Asparagus	FRESH	FRESH		
Bean		FRESH	FRESH	
Beet	STORED	FRESH	FRESH	STORED
Broccoli			FRESH	
Brussels			FRESH	STORED
Cabbage	STORED	FRESH	FRESH	STORED
Carrot	FRESH	FRESH	FRESH	STORED
Cauliflower		FRESH	FRESH	
Celeriac	STORED		FRESH	STORED
Celery		FRESH	FRESH	
Chard	FRESH	FRESH	FRESH	
Chicory, grn.			FRESH	STORED
Chicory, wit.			FRESH	STORED
Chin. Cab			FRESH	STORED
Claytonia	FRESH			FRESH
Corn		FRESH		
Cucumber		FRESH		
Dandelion	FRESH		FRESH	
Eggplant		FRESH	FRESH	
Endive		FRESH	FRESH	
Escarole		FRESH	FRESH	
Garlic	STORED	FRESH	FRESH	STORED
Kale	FRESH		FRESH	FRESH
Kohlrabi	FRESH	FRESH	FRESH	
Leek		FRESH	FRESH	STORED
Lettuce	FRESH	FRESH	FRESH	
Mache	FRESH			FRESH
Melon		FRESH		
Mizuna	FRESH	FRESH	FRESH	FRESH
Mustard	FRESH	FRESH	FRESH	
Onion, bulb	STORED	FRESH	FRESH	STORED
Onion, green	FRESH	FRESH	FRESH	
Parsley	FRESH	FRESH	FRESH	
Parsley Root			FRESH	STORED
Parsnip	FRESH			FRESH
Peas	FRESH	FRESH	FRESH	
Pepper		FRESH	FRESH	
Potato	STORED	FRESH	STORED	STORED
Pumpkin		FRESH	STORED	
Radicchio		FRESH	FRESH	
Radish	FRESH		FRESH	STORED
Rutabaga	STORED		FRESH	STORED
Sorrel	FRESH	FRESH	FRESH	
Spinach	FRESH		FRESH	FRESH
Squash, sum.		FRESH	FRESH	
Squash, winter	STORED		FRESH	STORED
Tomato		FRESH	FRESH	
Turnip	FRESH	FRESH	FRESH	STORED

ACKNOWLEDGEMENTS

WRITING A BOOK about how people can improve their lives is a nerve-wracking experience at best, not just in attempting to make sense of a mad world, but making sure your own suggestions don't turn out more mad. This book would not exist were it not for the encouragement of my old friend Victor Schmalzer. Much research was contributed by Heather Brown and Bridget Duffy, and continuous suggestion and input from my wife Candace. But mostly it took months of criticism and editing by my quietly insistent and always funny cohort Celine Little, who not only braved my writing but my cooking as well. And a big thanks to all the readers whose e-mails and letters regarding *A Reasonable Life* reassured me that all the effort was worthwhile.

—Ferenc Máté
NYC April, 2011

11. Edith Wharton, *The Last Asset* (Kessinger Publishing LLC, 2010).

14. W. Beran Wolfe, *How to Be Happy Though Human* (Farrar & Rinehart, 1931).

14. The New Shorter Oxford English Dictionary (Oxford University Press, 1993).

17. Bertrand Russell, British author, mathematician, & philosopher (1872–1970).

20. Dagobert Runes, *Dictionary of Philosophy* (Littlefield, Adams & Co., 168), 318.

20. W. Cole L. Phillips, *Random House Treasury of Humorous Quotations* (Random House Reference, 1999).

20. Mary Mackenzie, *Peaceful Living* (PuddleDancer Press, 2005).

22. Philip Schaff, *History of the Christian Church: Vol. II: From Constantine the Great to Gregory the Great A.D. 311–600* (Charles Scribner, 1867), 380 note 1.

22. Judith Shulevitz, *The Sabbath World* (Random House, 2010).

22. Judith Shulevitz, "Bring Back the Sabbath," *The New York Times Magazine*, March 2, 2003.

24. Shulevitz.

30. H. Jackson Brown, *Life's Treasure Book on Friendship* (Thomas Nelson, 2000).

31. Malcolm Gladwell, *Outliers* (Little, Brown and Company, 2008).

35. Great-Quotes.com Gledhill Enterprises, December 14, 2011 (http://www.great-quotes.com/quote/6760).

37. "History," http://www.whistlerblackcomb.com/about/history/index.htm.

40. Jack Rivers, "Rivers: How Many Good Friends Do You Have?" *The Milford Daily News*, May 1, 2010 (http://www.milforddailynews.com/opinion/x1195009618/Rivers-How-many-good-friends-do-you-have#axzz1Gar2Onry).

41. Pat Robertson, on "Anderson Cooper 360 Degrees," CNN, September 8, 2010, (http://archives.cnn.com/TRANSCRIPTS/1009/08/acd.01.html).

41. Timothy Egan, "Liars' Club," *The New York Times*, November 10, 2010.

42. Andrew Jacobs, "Bulldozers Meet Historic Chinese Neighborhood," *The New York Times*, July 20, 2010.

46. "Eco-towns target doubled by PM," *BBC News*, September 24, 2007.]

47. Easwaran, Eknath, *Gandhi the Man* (Nilgiri Press, 1997), 33.

54. Lewis Mumford, *The Urban Prospect* (Harcourt, Brace & World, 1968).

55. James Surowiecki, "The Pros and Cons of Financial Innovation," *The New Yorker*, May 17, 2010.

56. Robert Marks, *The Origins of the Modern World: A Global and Ecological Narrative* (Rowman & Littlefield, 2007).

57. Jeff Yeager, "10 Shocking Facts About Our World," *The Daily Green*, January 6, 2010 (http://www.thedailygreen .com/living-green/blogs/save-money/environmental -statistics-460110).

58. Lee Ann Obringer and Dave Roos, "How Mortgages Work," *HowStuffWorks.com*, (http://home.howstuffworks.com/ real-estate/mortgage2.htm).

59. George Packer, "The Ponzi State: Florida's foreclosure disaster," *The New Yorker*, February 9, 2009.

59. Ilyce Glink, "Underwater With Your Mortgage? So Are a Growing Number of Homeowners," *CBS Money Watch. com*, February 23, 2010. (http://moneywatch.bnet.com/ saving-money/blog/home-equity/underwater-with- your-mortgage-so-are-a-growing-number-of-homeown- ers/1699/)

60. Paul Bannister, "25 Fascinating Facts About Personal Debt," *Bankrate.com*, September 20, 2004 (http://www.bankrate. com/brm/news/debt/debtguide2004/debt-trivia1.asp).

65. Keith Hampton, Lauren Sessions, Eun Ja Her, Lee Rainie, "Social Isolation and New Technology," PewInternet.org, November 4, 2009.

66. "'Took all my pills, bye bye': Woman commits suicide on Facebook...and none of her 1,082 online friends help," *The Daily Mail*, January 6, 2011.

66. Gerard Celente, qtd. by Eric Slate, "Technoslave," *Adbusters*, April 21, 2008. (http://www.adbusters.org/magazine/77/ Technoslave.html).

69. "How You Fit Into the Tight Job Market," JobWeb.com, 2009 (http://www.jobweb.com/studentarticles.aspx?id=2121).

69. Clive Thompson, "The Ecology of Stress," *New York Magazine*, May 21, 2005.

72. Jeffrey Sachs, qtd. by Justin Gillis, "A Scientist, His Work and a Climate Reckoning," *The New York Times*, December 21, 2010.

73. John Vidal, "Niegra's Agony Dwarfs the Gulf oil spill. The US and Europe ignore it," *The Observer*, May 30, 2010.

73. Don Andy, "Sustainable Gaming 2 of 2—The Environment," DerNerdery.com, February 2011 (http://www.dernerdery.com/2011/02/sustainable-gaming).

83. Marc Levinson, "Living on the Edge," *Newsweek*, November 4, 1991.

83. Peter Kilborn, "Middle Class Feels Betrayed," *The New York Times*, January 12, 1992.

84. Steve Lohr, "Executives expect many 1991 Layoffs To Be Permanent. *The New York Times*, December 16, 1991

84. Daron P. Levin, "General Motors to cut 70,000 Jobs," *The New York Times*, December 18, 1991

84. Lisa W. Foderaro, "Hudson Valley Reels Under Impact of IBM Cuts," *The New York Times*, December 18, 1991

84. Peter T. Kilborn, "Bleak Economy Shattering Job Security in Banking," *The New York Times*, January 26, 1992.

84. "Worker Displacement, 01-03," *News*, United States Department of Labor, Bureau of Labor Statistics, July 30, 2004.

85. Peter Cohan, "With 15 million unemployed, thousands of middle class jobs go unfilled," *Daily Finance*, AOL Money and Finance, October 5, 2009.

85. Carol Morello and Dan Keating, "Recession Has Thrust

Millions More Into Poverty, Census Statistics Show," *The Washington Post*, September 11, 2009.

85. Cohan.

86. Nicholas Carr, *The Shallows: What the Internet is Doing to Our Brains* (W. W. Norton & Company, Inc., 2010)

87. "The Real Reasons You're Working So Hard…and what you can do about it," *Bloomberg Businessweek*, October 3, 2005

88. Michael Luo, "For Workers at Closing Plant, Ordeal Included Heart Attacks," *The New York Times*, February 25, 2010.

89. Luo.

89. Alice Park, "Shaken-Baby Cases Rose During the Recession," *TIME Magazine*, May 3, 2010.

90. Colin Turnbull, *The Mountain People*, Touchstone, July 2, 1987.

91. Paul Krugman, "The Third Depression," *The New York Times*, June 27, 2010.

91. B. Drummond Ayres, Jr., "American Voices: Fear for the Future-A Special Report; Shadow of Pessimism Eclipses a Dream," *The New York Times*, February 9, 1992.

95. Sam Williford, "German Growth Shows Lessons to Be Learned," *Economy in Crisis*, January 12, 2011 (http://www .economyincrisis.org/content/german-growth-outpaces -us-shows-lessons-be-learned).

95. David Leonhardt, "In Wreckage of Lost Jobs, Lost Power," *The New York Times*, January 19, 2011.

95. Katrin Bennhold, "Working (Part-Time) in the 21st Century," *The New York Times*, December 29, 2010.

100. *The Grapes of Wrath*, directed by John Ford, 1940.

106. Nancy Mann Jackson, "ESOP plans let founders cash out and employees cash in," CNNMoney.com, June 17, 2010.

108. Kelly K. Spors, "Top Small Workplaces 2008," *The Wall Street Journal*, February 22, 2009.

110. Richard Gunde, *Culture and Customs of China* (Greenwood Publishing Group, 2002).

113. Leslie Beck, "Top 25 Foods for Longevity," *The Globe and Mail*, January 4, 2011.

117. "The Impact of Home and Community Gardening in America," presentation, 5th Annual Garden Writers Web Teleconference, February 25, 2009.

117. "Favorite Pastimes," CNN.com (http://www.cnn.com/SPECIALS/2007/leisure/your.picks/index.html).

117. John D. Sutter, "Recession Gardens Trim Grocery Bills, Teach Lessons," CNN.com, April 1, 2009.

118. National Research Council, *Alternative Agriculture*, 34-35.

121. Liz Brody, "The Diet Years: Sure, it's a $35 billion industry..." *The Los Angeles Times*, February 1, 1996.

123. Jim Ewing, "Store-Bought Tomatoes Taste Like Cardboard? Here's Why," ClarionLedger.com, Gannett, April 1, 2011.

124 "UC Urges Use of Pesticide Alternatives in California Homes and Gardens," University of California Agriculture and Natural Resources, March 2006 (http://ucce1.ucdavis.edu).

126. Roger B. Swain, *Earthly Pleasures* (The Lyons Press, 1994).

126. Brian Halweil, "The Argument for Local Food," *World Watch Magazine*, World Watch Institute, May/June 2003, Vol. 16, No. 3.

127. "Declining Farmer Share of Retail Food Dollar Focus of

National Ag Day Event," Rocky Mountain Farms Union Website, March 20, 2000 (RMFU.org).

127. Johann Wolfgang von Goethe, qtd in *Civilization and its Discontents*, by Sigmund Freud, ed. By James Strachey (W.W. Norton & Company, Inc., 2005)

135. Nicolas D. Kristoff, "Pay Teachers More," *The New York Times*, March 12, 2011.

135. Linda Gorman, "Economic Explanations of Increased Obesity," The National Bureau of Economic Research (http://www.nber.org/digest/apr06/w11584.html)

136. "Understanding Adult Obesity," Weight-Control Information Network (http://www.win.niddk.nih.gov/publications/understanding.htm).

137. "Examining the Emotional Causes of Over-Eating," NHS Local, October 26, 2010. (http://nhslocal.nhs.uk/story/examining-emotional-causes-over-eating).

141. US Census Bureau (http://www.census.gov).

141. "Median and Average Square Feet of Floor Area in New Single-Family Houses Completed by Location," 2009 US Census Bureau.

141. "Crafton family enjoys rare closeness after seven years together at sea," by Steve Hendrix, *The Washington Post*, August 1, 2010.

146. "Can Apple Find More Hits Without Its Tastemaker?" by Steve Lohr, *The New York Times*, January 18, 2011.

146. *Highlights of Annual 2009 Characteristics of New Housing*, US Census Bureau

149. Mortgage calculator, From Wikipedia.com, updated March 2, 2011.

150. Johann Wolfgang von Goethe, quoted in *Civilization and its Discontents*

156. "Foreclosures Hit Record In September, More Than 100K Homes Seized," *The Huffington Post*, October 14, 2010.

156. LPS Mortgage Monitor, February 2011 Mortgage Performance Observations, Data as of January, 2011 Month-end.

156. Sarah Burgard, Jennie Brand, and James S. House "Perceived job insecurity and worker health in the United States," 2009 Social Science & Medicine, 69(5), 777-85.

159. Regional Energy Profile, U.S. Household Electricity Report, U.S. Energy Information Administration Independent Statistics and Analysis, July 14, 2005.

167. "Television, Internet and Mobile Usage in the U.S." A2/M2 Three Screen Report, 1st Quarter 2009, The Nielsen Company.

168. Victoria J. Rideout, M.A., Ulla G. Foehr, Ph.D., and Donald F. Roberts, Ph.D, "Generation M2: Media in the Lives of 8-to 18-Year-Old," Kaiser Family Foundation, January 2010.

176. Alan Mozes, "Cartoon Characters Sell Kids on Unhealthy Foods," *HealthDay News*, June 2011.

178. Carr.

184. Eric R. Kandel, *In Search of Memory: The Emergence of a New Science of Mind* (W. W. Norton & Company, Inc., 2007).

289. Ray Williams, "Is the 'Me Generation' less empathetic?" *Financial Post*, June 2010.

214. Brett Arends, "Why I Don't Want an iPad for Christmas" *The Wall Street Journal*, December 21, 2010.

215. Hilary Stout, "Effort to Restore Children's Play Gains Momentum," *The New York Times*, January 5, 2011.

229. Dr. Steven L. Paine and Andreas Schleicher, *What the U.S. Can Learn from the World's Most Successful Education Reform Efforts* (McGraw-Hill Research Foundation. Policy Paper: Lessons from PISA, 2010).

229. The Economic Impact of the Achievement Gap in America's Schools, Summary of Findings (McKinsey & Company, April 2009).

230. Bob Herbert ,"Outside the Casino," *The New York Times*, July 12, 2010.

230. Justin Snider, "Keys To Finnish Educational Success: Intensive Teacher-Training, Union Collaboration," *The Huffington Post*, March 17, 2011.

259. Clifford Thomas Morgan and Richard A. King, *Introduction to Psychology* (McGraw-Hill Inc., 1986).

241. "Mirror, mirror: A summary of research findings on body image" by Kate Fox (Social Issues Research Center, 1997).

246. The Social Animal: The Hidden Sources of Love, Character, and Achievement by David Brooks (Random House, March 8, 2011)

246. Allison Van Dusen, "How Depressed Is Your Country?" *Forbes*, February 16, 2007.

246. Trip Gabriel, "Mental Health Needs Seen Growing at Colleges", *The New York Times*, December 19, 2010.